A BOOK WITH A SPECIAL FEATURE!

PERFORATED PAGES

IF YOU SPOT YOUR BOSS IN ONE OF THE CHAPTERS, JUST:

1. PULL OUT THE CHAPTER.

2. FOLD ALONG THE LINE ON THE LAST PAGE OF THE CHAPTER.

3. WRITE IN YOUR BOSS'S NAME AND ADDRESS.

4. AFFIX A STAMP AND MAIL IT.

ABUSE 'EM AND LOSE 'EM

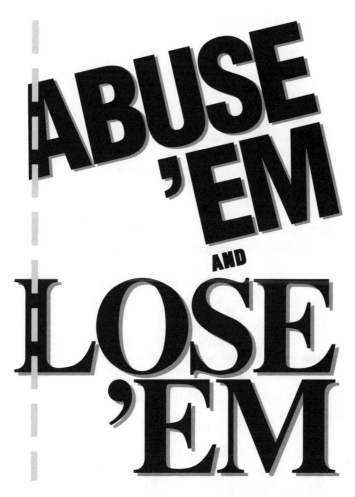

ABUSE 'EM AND LOSE 'EM

Eighteen leadership styles that were made in Hell

A practical guide for aspiring leaders by

Paul B. Malone III

Synergy Press
Annandale, Virginia

ABUSE 'EM AND LOSE 'EM

By Paul B. Malone III

Published by: Synergy Press
3420 Holly Road
Annandale, VA 22003 USA
(703) 573 0909

Book Design by Kevin Osborn, Arlington, Virginia
Printing by McNaughton & Gunn, Ann Arbor, Michigan

Library of Congress Cataloging in Publication Data.
Malone, Paul B. III
Abuse 'Em and Lose 'Em
1. Leadership
2. Management
3. Human Behavior
4. Organizational Behavior
Library of Congress Catalog Card Number 90-70734

ISBN 0-9616548-2-1 Softcover

FOREWORD

This book is about leadership—**getting people to do things—willingly.** To me, the subject is extremely important. Virtually everyone is involved in it—either leading others, being led or, in many cases, both. Leaders make a difference. Think of the long-term impact of Jesus Christ. Of course, he had an advantage. He had very special powers. Most of us have to settle for more mundane approaches.

This book is a sequel. It follows my first book, *Love 'Em and Lead 'Em*. The libraries are full of books on leadership. Most are complicated and even downright dull. I tried to make *Love 'Em and Lead 'Em* different—**fun to read**. My experience with the big publishers wasn't much fun. Leadership is serious business. They claimed that you can't mix levity and serious stuff. That's when I became Synergy Press. The World Headquarters of Synergy Press is the back of our garage. The "big boys" were wrong. We (my wife, Ann, and I) sold enough copies of *Love 'Em and Lead 'Em*—four printings as of now—to finance a swimming pool in our backyard.

Success leads to confidence; confidence leads to arrogance. I am convinced that the world now needs *Abuse 'Em and Lose 'Em*. I plan to employ the same style and format that I used with *Love 'Em and Lead 'Em*—cartoons, silly quotations, ridiculous names. I'd like very much for you to think about an important subject while, at the same time, being entertained. If you like *Abuse 'Em and Lose 'Em*, you should send for a copy of *Love 'Em and Lead 'Em*—our basement is full of them. If this book fails to touch your funny bone while transmitting a powerful message, send it back for a cheerful refund. However, don't expect a card from the Malones next Christmas.

There are two ways to learn about leadership. One approach is the **right** way. My view of the **right** way to lead people is contained in *Love 'Em and Lead 'Em*. Another approach is a focus on the **wrong** way. *Abuse 'Em and Lose 'Em* utilizes this approach. Eighteen chapters in this book describe eighteen corrupt and/or inept styles of leadership that turn subordinates **off**, demean them, and make their lives **less**. The final chapter contains six additional styles in less detail. You might spot your boss in one of the chapters; you might identify one of your subordinates; you might even discover yourself. If you do, shame on you! However, it's never too late to change. Each chapter includes suggestions relating to what actions you should consider in the event:

- You determine that your own style of leadership contains flaws described in the chapter.
- You discover that one of your subordinates displays undesirable tendencies.
- You find yourself working for a less-than-perfect boss.

Many people have misleading perceptions of themselves. Some bosses who view themselves with the qualities of Mary Poppins resemble Leona Helmsley or Lucrezia Borgia to others. Subordinates can't do much; they'll lose their jobs if they tell the truth. Horrible situations exist and persist because of lack of honest and candid communication.

At long last, this book provides a possible solution to this hitherto unsolvable dilemma. This book has a "gimmick" (my marketing professor friends prefer to call it a "marketing uniqueness," but I'll call it a "gimmick"). Notice that the pages of this book are perforated next to the spine. Note further that the last page of each chapter in Part B is essentially blank except for some lines, a box and a small amount of text. If you are reading *Abuse 'Em and Lose 'Em* on, for example, an airliner, and have no access to a photocopy machine, and spot your boss in one of the chapters, you can (1) tear out the chapter without completely destroying the book, (2) enter your boss's name and address on the appropriate lines (I suggest strongly that you omit a return address unless you're en route to Rio with plans to stay), (3) fold the chapter, staple and affix a stamp, and (4) mail the letter. Just think of your boss's appreciation for someone attempting to improve a realistic self-image! Further, think of the impact if the boss receives the identical chapter from several people! Perhaps Nicolae Ceausesçu or the Shah of Iran could have used feedback such as this. Perhaps *Abuse 'Em and Lose 'Em* can, in a small way, make this world a better place in which to live.

DISCLAIMER: THE AUTHOR DISCLAIMS ANY RESPONSIBILITY IN THE EVENT YOU MAIL A CHAPTER TO YOUR BOSS AND, AS A RESULT, LOSE YOUR JOB. DON'T SHOOT YOURSELF IN THE FOOT IF IT'S NOT POSSIBLE TO REMAIN ANONYMOUS!

"I COULD SPOT THAT HANDWRITING ANYWHERE! HAVE THAT WISE GUY, FESTUS FUNGUS, COME TO MY OFFICE NOW!"

DEDICATION

TO SOME VERY SPECIAL PEOPLE WHO HAVE CONTRIBUTED TO MY OPTIMISTIC VIEW OF HUMAN BEINGS:

ANN, ETHEL, PAUL IV, MARYLEE, PAT, DIANE, JIM, KATIE

ACKNOWLEDGMENTS

Leaders cannot exist in a vacuum. While I'll accept credit for this book if any is due, it certainly involved the inputs of many other generous and talented people. While writing this, I did a lot of **following**, I accepted a great deal of help, I "picked a bunch of brains". Very few "solo acts" exist in this complex world.

My first thanks go to my first and only wife of 37 years, Ann, who endured my five-month sabbatical while I wrote this book. Despite my outrageous hours and total preoccupation, she "kept the home fires burning" and provided outstanding advice at critical times.

Next, I must recognize the tremendous contributions of our daughter, Marylee, and her husband, Jim, who introduced this "no-tech" author to the intricacies of computer-assisted, desktop publishing. During their visits to our home and over the phone, long-distance, their responses to my screams of "help" were truly heroic. Further, one of Marylee's early suggestions regarding the basic organization of the book was critical to giving it focus.

Despite the pressing demands of his real estate career, a very special friend, Otis Moran (we made our first parachute jumps together many years ago), contributed many hours both to assist me with the computer and to provide many recommendations that are included in the book.

Another fine person and an outstanding proof reader, John Del Vecchio, spared no effort to ensure that *Abuse 'Em and Lose 'Em* was "squeaky clean" of errors. His contributions went far and above the "call of duty".

My sincere thanks go also to six friends–Father Jerome Daly, James Maloney, John Keeley, Ray Hanlein, Richard Wiles and Ken Morris–who reviewed an early draft and provided extremely valuable feedback that was incorporated into the final version.

Many associates at the School of Business and Public

Management of The George Washington University where I serve on the faculty contributed either directly or indirectly to this work. My thanks go to Dean Ben Burdetsky who approved the semester-long sabbatical that provided the time to write the book. I am also grateful to Professors Ernest Forman and David Brown for their assistance. Credit for the title of the book goes to Sam Goldenberg, one of my imaginative undergraduate students. My teaching assistant and President of the School's MBA Association at the time, Leah Fortino, contributed research support and some excellent advice. Very generous technical assistance was provided by Fred Ross and Samir Chebil at critical times.

Finally, my thanks go to my mother, Ethel Malone, for her extraordinary support as this book goes to press and our two sons, Major Paul Malone IV, U.S. Army, and Anthony Malone, whose recent experiences in "the trenches" leading others and being led provided insight included in *Abuse 'Em and Lose 'Em.*

CONTENTS

LEADERS

MANY ROLES MANY FACES

INTRODUCTION

This book is organized in three parts:

■ **PART A**, which consists of two chapters, provides you an explanation of what **LEADERSHIP** is and conceptualizes its effect on people. Further, Part A provides a very general description of the changing environment of leadership and a discussion of styles and philosophies available to those who have accepted the mantle of leadership.

■ **PART B**, which consists of eighteen chapters, describes styles and philosophies of leadership with "warts"; I consider them flawed. Each chapter focuses on a style—the result of the particular leader's personality, biases and idiosyncrasies—that affects the behavior of subordinates. I have exaggerated a bit and tried to be "cute" in order to make the reading light and entertaining, but be assured that leaders with some of these characteristics do exist. My objective is to make "bad examples" learning devices. It is generally acknowledged that mistakes often contribute to learning. However, if you make all of the world's mistakes yourself, you're likely to die as a very old failure. It would benefit you to be aware of the "pitfalls" that many leaders of the past AND THE PRESENT encounter and thus avoid them. If you are going to make mistakes, let them be original. When your turn to lead comes, do it right.

■ **PART C**, which consists of one chapter, provides my concluding thoughts and advice to others on the subject of leadership based on reflections of how flawed leaders can degrade the dignity of life and reduce the quality of the human condition. Further, the chapter suggests how *Abuse 'Em and Lose 'Em* might be put to productive use in enhancing leadership abilities.

PART A

BASIC CONCEPTS

CHAPTER ONE

A SLIPPERY CONCEPT: THE GLUE OF EXCELLENCE

"Leadership is the most observed and least understood phenomenon on earth."
J. M. Burus[1]

"Leadership is like the Abominable Snowman, whose footprints are everywhere but is nowhere to be seen."
Warren Bennis and Burt Nanus[2]

LEADERSHIP–getting people to do things–willingly. What is it? It's often confused with the term **MANAGEMENT.** Some consider the terms synonymous. I disagree. If management is an art, **leadership is a fine art.** When I was in the Vietnam War, I never saw anyone who was "managed" risk his life. Leadership was necessary–effective leadership. The problem with leadership is that it is a **slippery concept.** However, it is the **glue of excellence.** Management may be sufficient for organizations that (1) have no competition and (2) do not have to change in order to exist. All others need leadership–effective leadership.

COMMENT:

Some people are threatened by the concept of leadership. During the summer of 1989, I was presenting a paper at an international conference of academicians in Weimar, East Germany. An East German professor invited me to his home. During our conversations, he indicated an interest

in my writing activities. I told him about my first book on leadership, *Love 'Em and Lead 'Em*. He paused thoughtfully and asked, "Why would anyone want to write a book on that subject?" Initially, I thought he was pulling my leg, but he was dead serious. He continued, "We Germans would rather be governed by an impersonal bureaucracy than by some charismatic leader." I guess he had a point. Not more than fifteen miles away was the Buchenwald Prison Camp, a grisly legacy of Adolph Hitler, a charismatic leader.

Things have changed significantly in East Germany since my visit. The "impersonal bureaucracy" that provided some degree of "comfort"–at great cost–has been replaced by God knows what.

Some readers of this book are going to complain that it is written by an academician who is no longer "in the trenches" and who has an idealistic and totally unrealistic perception of people. They may be right, but look around at what's happening to the world. The Communist System, attractive in theory with the needs of the people "satisfied" but **based on a total mistrust of people**, is being declared bankrupt. No one is really sure what will replace it. I suggest that a system that views people in a more positive light–built in the image and likeness of God–is worth a try. If such a "Grand Experiment" is to have a chance, leaders who give a damn about people must emerge. Maybe books like *Abuse 'Em and Lose 'Em* will help this to happen.

LEADERSHIP: HOW TO DESCRIBE IT

As mentioned previously, the concept of leadership is somewhat hard to comprehend or define. When words prove inadequate, analogies and illustrations can help.

Leadership: A Chemical Reaction

I liken the leadership process to a chemical combination, WITH A SPECIAL TWIST. Most chemical combinations conclude with totally predictable results. **Nothing is totally predictable when people are involved.**

The first thing essential for the leadership process is a setting or an environment. Our analogy, based on a "chemical combination", uses the test tube on page 6. Each organization provides an environment within which people operate.

Next, we pour in the basic ingredients of leadership–the people. Note that, for convenience, I've drawn people as balls; the bigger the balls, the greater the power. Obviously, the leader in this case is the biggest ball of all.

Now we apply heat–the heat associated with any task on page 7. Most organizations must do something if they are to exist. Note that the people churn about as they interact. Some don't like what they see and get out.

As in every chemical combination, there comes a final reaction. This applies to leadership too. Most leaders would like this to be favorable (the smile in the cloud at the left)–a desirable condition if there are to be further applications of heat. **HERE'S THE RUB REGARDING LEADERSHIP.** There's just no guarantee that the reaction will be favorable with all of the people **NO MATTER HOW GOOD YOU ARE.** Since each person is unique, it is very likely that the "chemistry" between the leader and one or more subordinates will be unfavorable.

COMMENT:

What's the message here? Even the world's greatest leader must be prepared for rejection; you can't win them all; be prepared to be unloved. If you need continual approval, work alone unless you can't stand yourself.

CHEMISTRY OF HUMAN INTERACTION

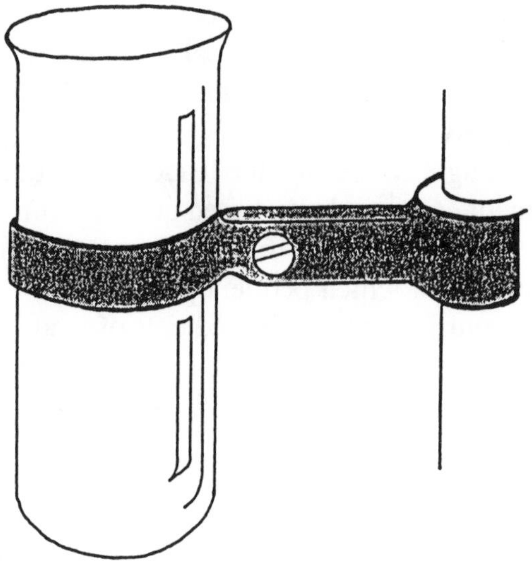

THE ENVIRONMENT

POUR IN THE PEOPLE

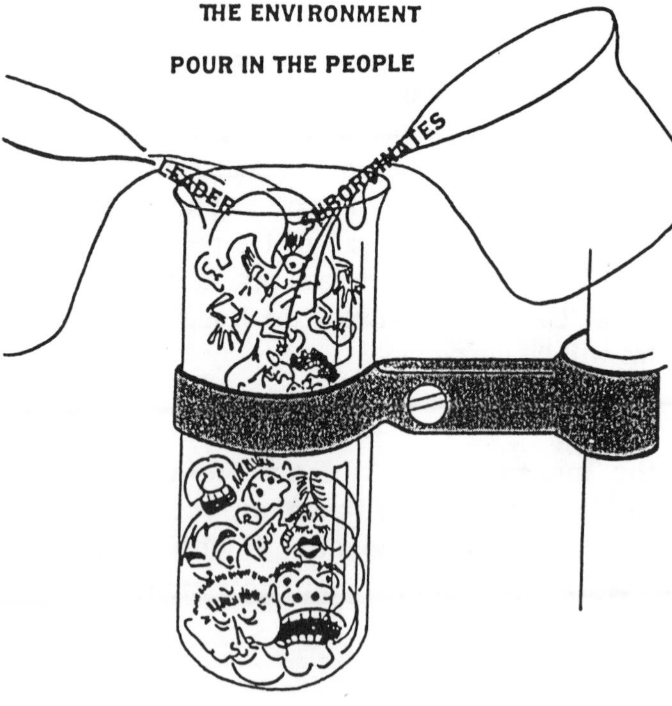

A Slippery Concept: The Glue of Excellence

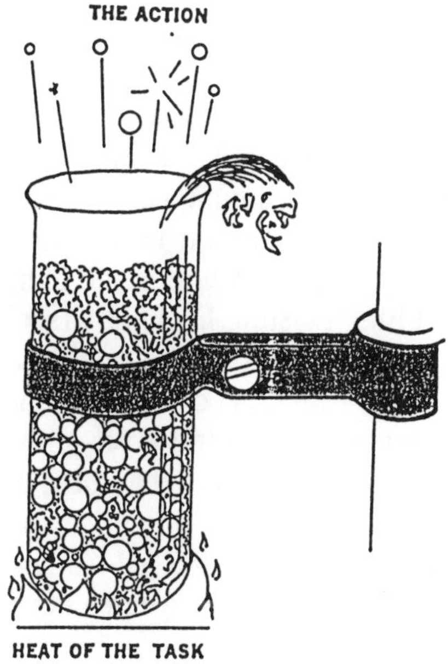

Leadership: The Effect on Others

Let's take another look at the concept, this time focusing on the behavior of one human being. Please follow my thoughts as I examine a person from a unique perspective–**the range of human endeavor**. Note that this range is portrayed in the diagram on page 9. This person operates within the identified limits. In fact, he goes through life "twisting his knob" (see the knob–you've got a knob too but don't look for it; you might disfigure yourself). He sets his knob on "full speed", "half speed" or "no speed" depending on how much or little he is stimulated by a particular environment. Note also that his behavior is influenced by a spring. This is the spring of motivation that gives him the energy to react. Most people who have encountered some success in life have strong springs. Sadly, some who have never had reason to hope have weak springs.

Let's take our person through a few experiences. First, note our hero on page 10 who enters an environment, for example a workplace, is turned **off**, and dials **"no speed"**. Almost always, the result is **mediocrity**. Most bosses would not tolerate this person.

In another situation, the person enters the workplace, examines what's in it for him, dials **"half speed"** and achieves **adequacy**–just enough to get by. Here's where I'd like to make a point. Most people who are **managed, treated like inanimate cogs in an impersonal machine,** operate at **"half speed"**. Ironically, many bosses not only **tolerate** this but also **condone** it. I'm convinced that much of the American work force is operating at **"half speed"**. They are **physically** involved in their work, but their **minds** and **hearts** are elsewhere.

I'm obviously saving the best for the last. Here, on page 11, our subject enters the workplace, examines the situation, is turned **on**, and dials **"full speed"**. Usually, the result is **excellence**. The person is **physically, mentally** and **emotionally** involved in the situation. You can tell by the smile on his face. I've dealt with a

THE RANGE OF HUMAN ENDEAVOR

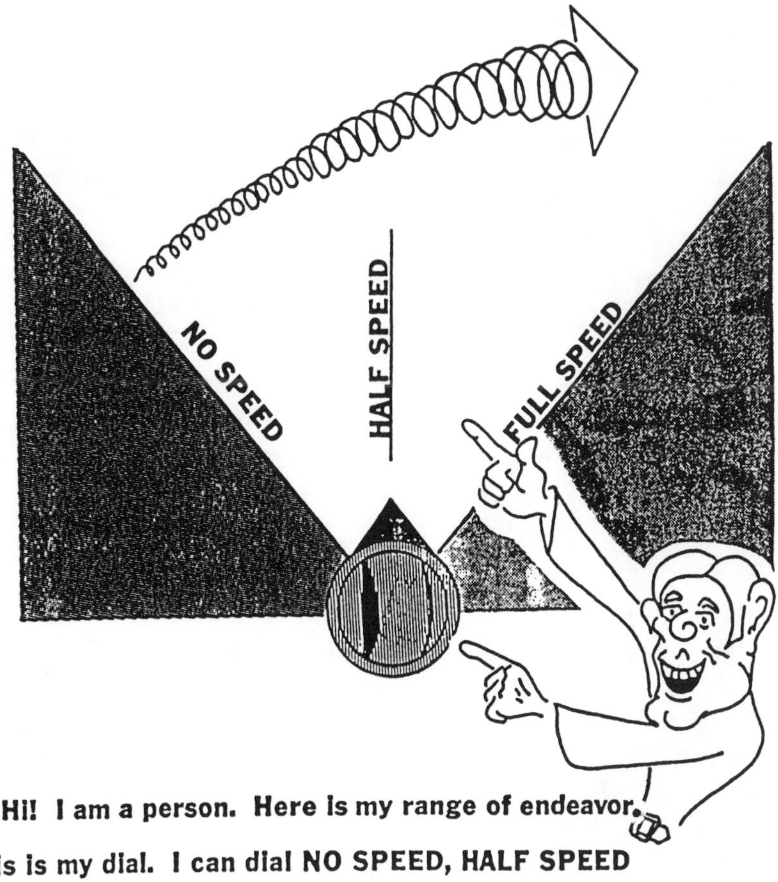

"Hi! I am a person. Here is my range of endeavor. This is my dial. I can dial NO SPEED, HALF SPEED or FULL SPEED. Up top is my spring of motivation."

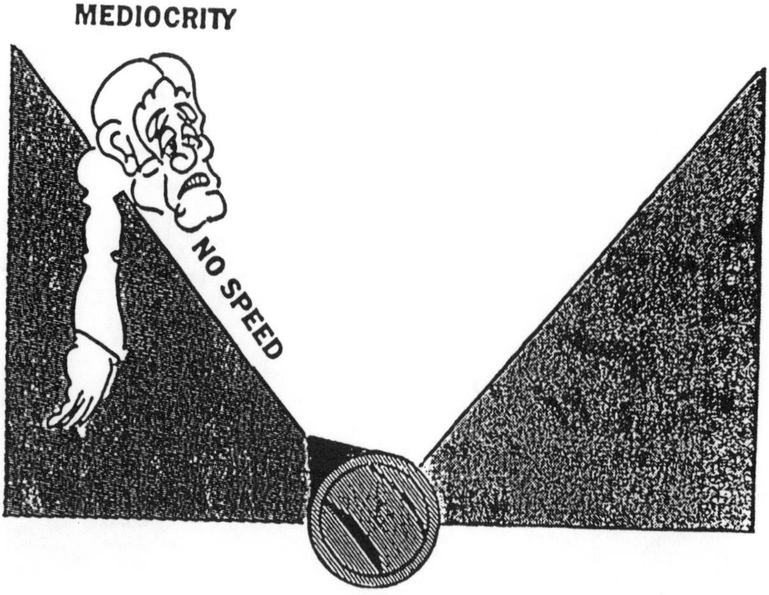
MEDIOCRITY
NO SPEED

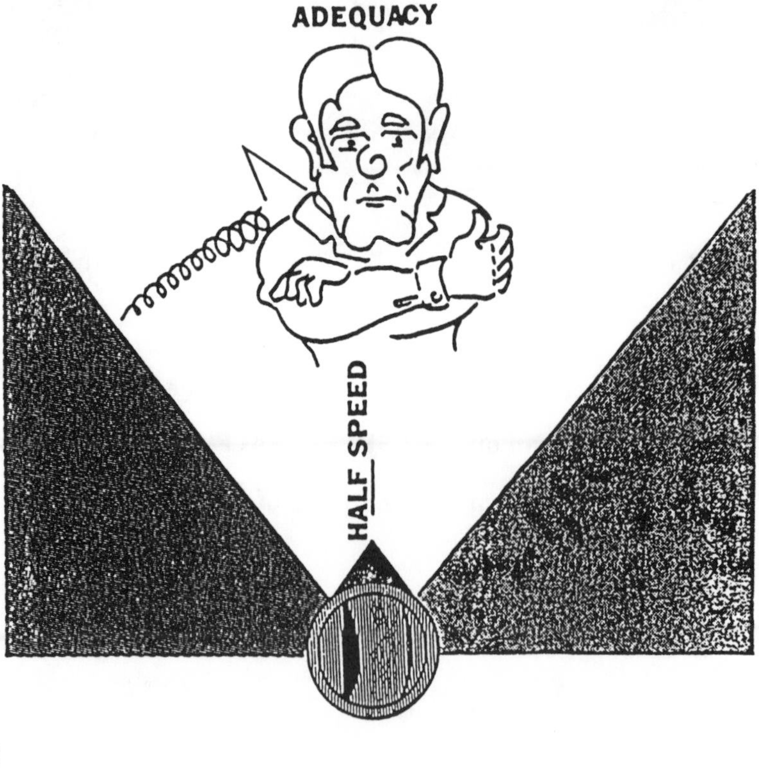
ADEQUACY
HALF SPEED

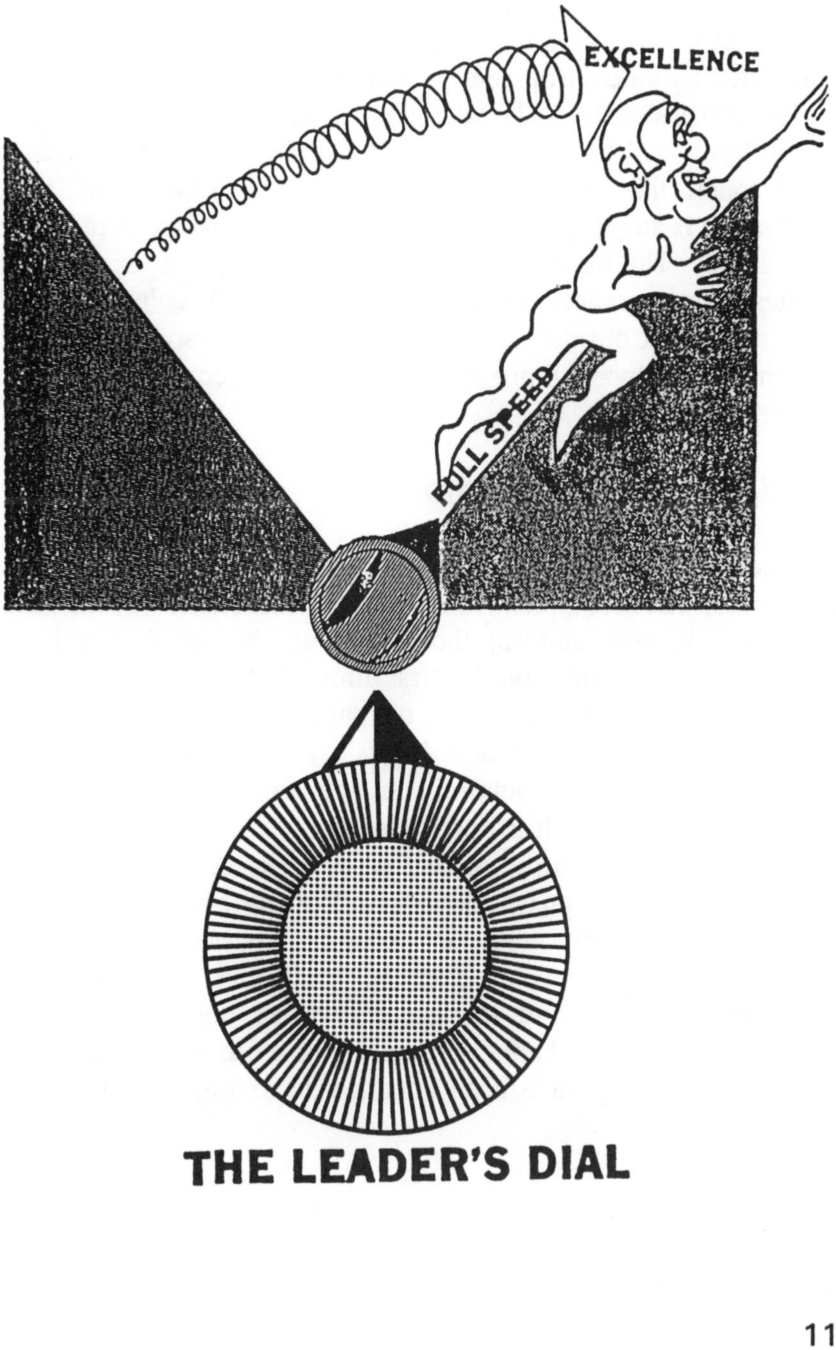

THE LEADER'S DIAL

variety of types of people including some who were not particularly sophisticated. I've **never** found anyone who wanted to be associated with **mediocrity. Excellence is largely a state of mind stimulated by an environment provided by the leader.**

This illustrates the real challenge of leadership. Notice that the leader has a dial too–a big one. The problem is that the leader can't touch the subordinate's dial–only the subordinate can. **Motivation is an internal force. The only person who can motivate you is you.** The leader's task is to turn his dial in a manner that **creates an organizational environment where people voluntarily dial "full speed".** Considering the fact that every person is different and there are always limits on resources, this requires talent and commitment.

Leadership: The Results

Another way to measure leadership is by what it accomplishes. Remember that accomplishment has two dimensions: (1) the tasks that are achieved, and (2) the effects on the people involved. **Managers** tend to focus on the first dimension only.

Take a look at the cartoons on page 13. The first cartoon illustrating **unsuccessful leadership** is a bit obvious. The leader points the way and the subordinates tell him to go suck an egg. The only tangible result is open rebellion.

Let's now refer to the second cartoon, **successful leadership.** Note that the subordinates do respond to the leader's direction. That's fine but, to my mind, not enough. What leaders should be seeking is a step beyond–**effective leadership.** Not only do subordinates comply with the leader's wishes, but something else that's very important happens–**they feel a sense of satisfaction in the process.** They have been conditioned to want to follow the leader again.

LEADERSHIP RESULTS

UNSUCCESSFUL LEADERSHIP

SUCCESSFUL LEADERSHIP

EFFECTIVE LEADERSHIP

SUCCESSFUL PLUS

"THAT WAS GREAT, BOSS. LET'S DO IT AGAIN.
WE'LL FOLLOW YOU ANYWHERE!"

COMMENT:

What's the overall message here? First, leadership effectiveness is influenced by a series of "chemistries"—psychological reactions, all unpredictable, between leaders and subordinates. Second, leaders create organizational environments that contribute to subordinate reactions—"no speed", "half speed" or "full speed". Again, each reaction is unique. Third, leadership results have two dimensions: (1) what is achieved, and (2) the effects on the people involved. Effective leadership requires positive results in <u>both</u> dimensions.

Note that the basic ingredients of leadership, the people, are all unique. Here's where leading people becomes challenging; leaders <u>should not</u> deal with each person identically. While this complicates the leader's task, it certainly adds to the "spice of life". Wouldn't things be dull if everyone in the world wanted to be a—<u>proctologist</u>? If nothing else, think of what that would do to eye-to-eye contact!

COMMENT:

The chapters beginning with Chapter Three describe some styles of leadership that I consider flawed. I will be referring to terms and concepts that may otherwise be unfamiliar to the reader. For that reason, Chapter Two contains a discussion of the environment of leadership with a particular focus on the United States. I will be "skimming the surface" and generalizing a lot. I realize that generalizing leaves gaps and allows for inaccuracies, but it's the best I can do considering the scope of this book. I will be borrowing some material from my first book on leadership, *Love 'Em and Lead 'Em*. If you've read that book, you might want to move on to Chapter Three. If you haven't, I suggest that you read Chapter Two.

NOTES

[1]Bernard M. Bass, *Stogdill's Handbook of Leadership* (New York: The Free Press, 1981), p. 5.

[2]Warren Bennis and Burt Nanus, *Leaders* (New York: Harper & Row, 1985), p. 20.

CHAPTER TWO

LEADERSHIP: WHAT'S NEW AND DIFFERENT?

"Many of the values that influence our behavior are products of the Industrial Revolution. We now live in the Post-Industrial Society with different values, particularly those that apply to people." (BIG BOOK, Small Paul to the People Squeezers, 29:66)

"A new model of leadership is needed. . . . To determine what kind of leader we need, we must understand how we are changing and why old models of leadership no longer serve."

Michael Maccoby[1]

WHAT IS THE SOCIAL ENVIRONMENT OF LEADERSHIP IN THE UNITED STATES?

Many of the original emigrants from Europe to the United States were seeking something called "freedom" and escape from the oppression of despotic leaders who derived their power from "divine right" or inflexible class systems. Thanks to the bountiful natural resources of the American continent, many found precisely what they were looking for. They shoved the Indians out of the way, carved out farms and lived in free isolation without much need for leaders. Some, recognizing the need for someone else to do the "dirty work", sent to Africa for slaves. "Freedom" applied to some; others didn't benefit much. The Anglo-Saxon Protestants were the first "ins"; other European groups such as the Irish, Italians and Swedes were initially "outs"; black people were the "way outs". The philosophy of individual private enterprise (great for the "ins") applied; the *laissez-faire* doctrine of government (he who governs least governs best) prevailed.

The advent of the Industrial Revolution led to major change. Many people voluntarily left the isolated freedom of farms and moved to the cities to work in factories. Large organizations emerged. Like it or not, people in factories became subordinates to other people. Some gained great wealth; some lived like dogs–but they were "free" (or were they?). A great Civil War was fought. Presumably, the black person was emancipated.

American energies then turned to the West with all of its opportunities and resources. There was enough "slack" in the system to allow the *laissez-faire* approach to continue. Those with the wealth and the vision to build great business empires were admired as heroes–their imperfections were tolerated. After all, they contributed to greater wealth and more jobs.

America ended its isolation by participating in World War I. After the war, Americans turned to "good times" followed by a Great Depression. The devastating period of the Depression led to a major reorientation in national policy. It was determined that unfettered private enterprise led to intolerably gross abuses. With the New Deal of President Franklin D.Roosevelt came the end of *laissez-faire* government. It was determined that the power of leaders must be limited by legislation–federal, state and local. It was decided that government had a role in redistributing wealth, that the inequities of the private enterprise system were too severe. Later on, society concluded that many of the "outs" of the population–minorities, women, old people, handicapped people–should have opportunities equal to the "ins".

Culturally, many Americans are suspicious of leaders. They

enjoy looking for flaws and subjecting leaders to ridicule. Americans tend to be litigious people; count our number of lawyers. American leaders run severe risks when they consider themselves "above the law" (note Richard Nixon). While Americans seek leadership in times of crisis, they are ready to identify a "human sacrifice", often the leader, when things go wrong. Personal accountability is very important to most Americans.

HOW HAS THE NATURE OF WORK CHANGED?

With the possible exception of the Garden of Eden, Man has always had to do some work in order to live. Much of this work was classified as "dirty work"–sweaty, arduous, repetitive, boring–anything but entertaining. Some enterprising people came up with a "great" idea: "Why not get someone else to do the 'dirty work'?" This idea led to a bunch of invasions, wars, crusades (call them what you like) in quest of, among other things, slaves. With this situation, a few people could live in the lap of luxury while the rest barely survived and did the "dirty work". Since work had to be done, the big deal was finding **someone else** to do it. Those who did were upper class. Naturally, they fought hard to keep this status.

Work in agrarian societies, where most people **tilled the soil**, was relatively simple–and "dirty". However, there could be a degree of freedom and independence–people could scratch out enough to eat even in bad times.

Then came the Industrial Revolution where most people were engaged in **producing things** in factories. The upper class, those with the wealth to invest in the factories, remained. There was plenty of "dirty work" to do at the bottom. Much of this "dirty work" was intentionally designed to be very simple and routine on assembly lines so that simple, uneducated people could perform without much preparation or serious thinking. Initially, this work was done by the lower class. Later, with the help of legislation and the unions, some of these people emerged into the middle class. Further, another middle class group appeared–those who coordinated the efforts of the workers for the owners, the supervisors and managers. Additionally, increasing affluence and the explosion of knowledge contributed to the growing need for highly trained specialists called professionals. More and more, work was being performed by the mind rather than the muscle, at least for those who had the mental skills and the opportunity to use them. Some work took on new meaning. It was no longer "dirty". In fact, it was rewarding, meaningful–even fun. This type of work gave people status in a society that valued the Work Ethic (work is, by its basic nature, "good").

In the United States, the Industrial Revolution has been replaced by the Post-Industrial Society where the majority of the population **provides services.** While there's still some "dirty work" to do, much of it is being done by machines. Education and skill are replacing physical strength as the essential prerequisites for good jobs. Even many of the entry-level jobs require that the employee be able to read, write and compute numbers. The law now requires that all groups, including women, minorities and older people, have the same opportunity as the traditional "ins" to work. The basic values of the Industrial Revolution–centralization, standardization, a blind reverence for bigness–are being challenged as products and services are provided according to unique customer specifications.[2] In some cases, people who, in the past, have performed their routine tasks without thought are being asked for ideas and opinions. Some jobs allow for the cottage industry approach–working at home or in isolated areas and linked to the boss electronically. Recognizing that the assembly line approach has contributed to worker alienation, some bosses are seeking to "enrich" jobs by focusing on the following five core job characteristics:

- Job Significance: The degree to which the worker considers his or her work important.

- Job Identity: The degree to which the worker can relate to a complete product or task.
- Skill Variety: The scope of different activities required by the job.
- Autonomy: The amount of freedom allowed the worker as he or she performs the job.
- Feedback from Job: The degree to which the worker is informed about the quality of his or her work.[3]

As the body of available knowledge expands, people specialize, some super-specialize. Education becomes a lifelong rather than a one-time activity as the "half-life" of much knowledge is reduced to but a few years. Increasing affluence has contributed to a huge middle class–a group that, while not basking in the lap of unlimited luxury, has the opportunity to live enriching and rewarding lives. Many of these people expect satisfactions WHILE AT WORK.

HOW HAVE ORGANIZATIONS CHANGED?

In primitive societies, people tended to live in small tribes. As things became more "organized", governments appeared. Some, such as the Roman Empire, were big; most were more modest. Since communications were very slow, control of other people over great distances was tenuous at best. There were some major efforts at organizing. Most of these were armies designed to kill or conquer some "enemy". In almost all cases, leaders were determined by an approach related to "divine right".

Typically, business activities were conducted on a small scale–craftsmen working in homes or small groups. Barter was common since the financial system wasn't well organized.

The Industrial Revolution brought with it the opportunity and the necessity for commercial bigness. People were lured from the isolation of their farms to the cities where the factories were. The concepts of economies of scale and the specialization of labor were introduced. The selection of leaders was still arbitrary–based largely on the prevailing class system. The system was relatively simple. The leaders, the upper class, did the thinking and gave orders; the followers, the lower class, obeyed without thinking or lost their jobs. There were few who challenged this system, at least initially.

As the Industrial Revolution progressed and some of the inter-class barriers began to crumble while democratic ideas got their start, a new concept appeared–THE BUREAUCRACY. The "big deal" of bureaucracy is the idea that people should be rewarded (paid and promoted) based on demonstrated **merit** rather than **family bloodlines**. Bureaucratic organizations have some other characteristics:

- They're usually big.
- They're usually organized by **function**. People are encouraged to specialize by function.
- Decision making is usually centralized (done at the top since only those at the top are responsible for all functions). For this reason, decision making is often a slow process.
- Levels of hierarchy are important; most communication is done formally through the "chain of command" (vertical lines in the organization chart).
- They have lots of rules, regulations and procedures.
- They provide for employee security against the capricious and arbitrary behavior of bosses.[4]

Bureaucratic organizations served the Industrial Revolution well. They are ideal for repetitious, routine operations. However, they tend to founder when the situation becomes dynamic rather than static. Therein lies the major limitation of a bureaucracy–**it does not respond readily to change.**

The Post-Industrial Society has brought with it new demands on organizations. What are needed are organizational concepts that are adaptable to change regardless of the size of organization. All sorts of approaches–matrix organizations, temporary task forces, Toffler's concept of "ad-hocracy"[5]–are being tried with varying degrees of success. Big organizations still exist. In fact, some are getting bigger with mergers, acquisitions and the like. However, there is great opportunity for smaller, more maneuverable organizations where decisions can be made quickly and where the organizational environment is **very personal** rather than **impersonal**. Big organizations often leave "niches of opportunity" for the little ones–opportunities to provide consulting, maintenance, insurance and similar services not considered cost-effective by the big organizations. Some of these "niches" provide ideal opportunities for individuals who are disenchanted with big organizations and would like to be self-employed.

HOW HAVE PEOPLE CHANGED?

The honest answer to this question is that they haven't. However, we know more about people now than we used to. My focus is going to be on people in advanced Post-Industrial Societies. Their behavior is quite different when compared to people in earlier times or people in other stages of development. There are reasons for this. I'll try to explain why in a few paragraphs. A complete treatment of the subject would require volumes.

Interest and related research focusing on why people behave as they do in the working environment have been generally confined to the Twentieth Century. An American, Frederick Taylor, developed an Economic Man approach to motivation. The approach was pretty simple. Man needs tangible things, notably money, in order to live. In order to get him to work harder, you offer him what he wants–more money.[6]

The world-famous psychologist, Abraham Maslow (**almost everybody's heard of him!**), agreed up to a point. He concluded that Man has extremely strong **basic** needs for food, water, shelter, sex and security but that, when these are satisfied, he has **higher-level** needs for belonging, esteem (self-esteem and the esteem of others) and, finally, something he called self-actualization (being everything you can be). Maslow called Man a "wanting animal" who is always seeking to satisfy needs. Once a need is satisfied, he's looking for something else, frequently a higher-level need.[7]

COMMENT:

If you ever discover totally satisfied employees, check their pulses. According to Maslow, they're DEAD!

Another eminent authority, Frederick Herzberg, developed a two-factor theory of motivation. According to Herzberg, you can eliminate employee dissatisfaction by satisfying their **basic level** needs (provide adequate pay, decent working conditions, good supervision). However, again according to Herzberg, these people will be **"neutral"** (neither dissatisfied nor motivated). If you want them to be "motivated" (committed to improving performance; intellectually and emotionally involved in their work), you must then proceed to satisfy **higher-level** needs (responsibility, recognition, the opportunity to grow and develop, interesting and challenging jobs). Factors associated with **basic-level** needs are called **extrinsic**; factors associated with **higher-level** needs are called **intrinsic.**[8] Most **extrinsic** needs are satisfied away from the workplace; most **intrinsic** needs are satisfied while working.

Obviously, I have barely scratched the surface of the knowledge in this subject area. Summarized below are some points regarding most people in affluent, Post-Industrial societies that I think leaders should consider:

- Each person is a unique human being with a unique set of attitudes, values, goals and expectations. What turns one person on may be of no interest to another.
- Each person is seeking to satisfy personal needs. When needs are satisfied, other, often higher-level needs become important. If rewards offered by

leaders are to be effective, they must relate to the individual's personal value system at a particular time.

- Each person is looking for the "best available deal"—something better. If one employer can't offer what the person wants, perhaps another can.
- Each person expects to be treated with dignity and respect. Most deserve it; those who don't probably should be institutionalized.
- As the person matures, he or she seeks greater freedom. However, he will give up some of that freedom in order to earn a living. If he feels that the "price is too high," he will resent it.
- A person who is treated like a child will eventually behave like a child.
- Mature, educated people seek responsibility; many are both innovative and creative.
- Mature, educated people are most effective when they feel that they have some control over their lives. They commit themselves to decisions they helped determine.
- Some people are content to engage in routine, repetitive and monotonous work. Often they satisfy their higher-level needs outside of the workplace (church, social clubs, hobbies).
- People are attracted to leaders who share their own value systems.
- People are threatened by change (even when it is obviously necessary).

WHAT STYLES OF LEADERSHIP ARE AVAILABLE?

If you'll accept my definition of leadership—**getting people to do things—willingly**—two key words come out—PEOPLE and THINGS. To a large degree, leadership is a balancing act as indicated in the cartoon on page 27.

The leader has two primary responsibilities: (1) to get the assigned job done, and (2) to take care of subordinates. Often, these concerns are in conflict. The leader's determination of relative priorities for each of these two responsibilities influences his leadership style. Remember that the leader's style has two dimensions: (1) the style the leader believes he or she uses, and (2) the leader's style as viewed by subordinates. I contend that the second dimension is more significant than the first. Many leaders have distorted views of how they appear to others. That's the reason for the perforated pages in this book; GIVE YOUR BOSS A BLAST OF REALITY, IF APPROPRIATE!

Rensis Likert identified four basic styles of leadership that are described briefly below:

- **EXPLOITATIVE AUTHORITATIVE**–The leader who makes all of the decisions himself (authoritative) and treats his subordinates in an abusive manner–like dirt.
- **BENEVOLENT AUTHORITATIVE**–The leader who makes all of the decisions himself (authoritative) but treats his subordinates in a kindly manner–very much like children. The term **PATERNALISTIC** applies to this style of leadership.
- **CONSULTATIVE**–The leader who asks subordinates their opinions regarding decisions but makes the decisions himself.
- **PARTICIPATIVE**–The leader who actually shares decision-making authority with subordinates (lets them make some decisions) while retaining responsibility for the decisions of all.[9]

I'm going to add another style not identified by Likert. This is known as **LAISSEZ-FAIRE** leadership. This type of leader essentially allows subordinates to "do their own thing" with the leader intervening only when they need help.

THE LEADER'S BALANCING ACT

COMMENT:

Experts tend to agree that, as societies mature and people become more sophisticated, leadership styles should become more participative. However, rest assured that there are some Exploitative Authoritative leaders around, and some of them are doing very well. I contend that their chances of success are less than they used to be. Personally, if I had my way, I'd put some of them in jail for abusing power and making the lives of their subordinates less satisfying and rewarding.

Before I close this discussion, let me address a few leadership-related terms that will come up later in the book. The first of these is the word **power**, <u>the ability to attain dominance over others</u>. If, as indicated previously, people are basically selfish and interested only in satisfying their <u>personal</u> needs, how does one get them to do things the <u>organization</u> needs? Leaders have **power**. They use this to get subordinates to engage in activities needed by the organization. They acquire power in one of three ways: (1) it's given to them by others, (2) they buy it (Jack Kent Cooke), or (3) they grab it. There are six basic sources of power that are listed below. Note that power exists because **subordinates** (not the bosses) recognize it.

- COERCIVE POWER–The ability of the leader to punish.
- REWARD POWER–The ability of the leader to reward.
- LEGITIMATE POWER–The ability of the leader to influence others, based on his or her status in the organization.
- EXPERT POWER–The ability of the leader to influence others, based on expertise possessed by the leader.
- REFERENT POWER–The ability of the leader to influence others, based on the power of his or her personality. The term *charisma* refers to referent power.
- INFORMATION POWER–The ability of the leader to

influence others based on the exclusive access to certain information.[10]

Finally, the following two terms come up frequently when discussing the subject of leadership.

- **AUTHORITY**–The right of the leader to make decisions or to require or prohibit certain actions.
- **RESPONSIBILITY**–The liability or accountability owed by the leader to the organization and the subordinates.

Note that **AUTHORITY** can be delegated (passed down to others); **RESPONSIBILITY** cannot. **The leader is always responsible for everything the organization does or fails to do.**

HOW SHOULD I LEAD?

That's the subject of my first book, *Love 'Em and Lead 'Em.* There are all sorts of theories on leadership (all with different conclusions) and plenty of people who will try to tell you how. Here's my approach in a nutshell.

First, recognize two facts:

(1) **It's tougher and more demanding to lead now than in the past.** Subordinates demand more of leaders. Society and the organizations are more complex. Leaders must serve as "engines of change" rather than maintainers of the *status quo.*

(2) **Participative leadership–sharing decision-making power with subordinates–is no longer an option; IT'S A MUST!** Most people resent being denied the opportunity to think and express their opinions at work. Further, with so much essential knowledge available, no one can be an "expert" in everything. Leaders must rely on the knowledge of others. The leader's basic choice is how much power to delegate.

Second, each person is a unique individual with unique attitudes, values, goals and aspirations. **The leadership style that works best for you is a function of your personality.** If you are to be an effective leader, you should:

(1) Analyze yourself to identify your uniqueness.
(2) Determine how your uniqueness affects other people.
(3) Develop a personal philosophy of leadership—a general statement of who you are, what values you have and how you plan to lead others.
(4) Share that philosophy with your subordinates and live by it. Let your subordinates know if and when you decide to change your basic philosophy.

Part C of *Love 'Em and Lead 'Em* provides a guide to assist in developing your philosophy. I provided my own philosophy just to serve as an example recognizing that, since no two people are identical, no two philosophies should be the same. My philosophy is listed below. It's written in biblical form to amuse the reader, but I believe in it. I'd like to think I lived by it—at least most of the time.

MALONE'S COMMANDMENTS OF LEADERSHIP

1. **Thou shalt develop a personal philosophy of leadership, share part of it with thy subordinates and live by it, recognizing that thou canst fool none of the people none of the time.**

2. **Thou shalt view thy subordinates as the children of God and behave accordingly in thy exercise of power, recognizing that power corrupts and thou art corruptible.**

3. **Thou shalt not bring sadness and gloom unto the workplace. Instead, thou shalt endeavor to enrich the life of each subordinate thou toucheth.**

4. **Thy mind shalt dwell in the future whenever possible. Thou shalt not make a decision that a subordinate could**

make just as well.

5. Thou shalt not direct thy subordinates without explaining WHY.

6. Thou shalt tolerate and even encourage some degree of conflict, disagreement and error, and combat the afflictions of doppelgangeritis, numberungus and pole-vaulting over mouse droppings.

7. Thy hand shalt include both a palm and knuckles. Thou shalt reward frequently and in public BUT thou shalt also possess the innards to punish in private with blinding speed and surgical skill.

8 .While thou shalt maintain some "psychological distance" from thy subordinates, thou shalt make thyself available to those in trouble, offering thy hand, thy ear, thy heart and thy handkerchief but never thy money. In the process, thou shalt resist the temptation to play God or psychiatrist unless thou art properly anointed or qualified.

9. Thou art responsible for everything thy organization does or fails to do. When things are "gangbusters", thou shalt step back and introduce thy subordinates. When everything turns brown, thou shalt step forward and take thy licks.[11]

CONCLUSION

There are as many styles of leadership as there are people on this earth who lead. Some are effective; some are not. Some contribute to organizational success; some do not. Some turn subordinates **on**; some turn them **off**. In the following chapters, let's take a look at a variety of styles and their effects on organizations and their people.

NOTES

[1]Michael Maccoby, *The Leader* (New York: Simon and Schuster, 1981), p. 17.

[2]Alvin Toffler, *The Third Wave* (New York: Morrow, 1980).

[3]J. R. Hackman and G. R. Oldham, *Work Redesign* (Reading, MA: Addison-Wesley Publishing Company, 1980), p. 77.

[4]Max Weber, *The Theory of Social and Economic Organization* (New York: Oxford University Press, 1947).

[5]Alvin Toffler, *Future Shock* (New York: Random House, Inc., 1970), pp. 125, 142, 146.

[6]Frederick W. Taylor, *The Principles of Scientific Management* (New York: Harper & Brothers, 1911).

[7]Abraham Maslow, *Motivation and Personality* (New York: Harper & Row, 1970).

[8]Frederick Herzberg, "One More Time: How Do You Motivate Employees?" *Harvard Business Review*, January-February, 1968, pp. 53-62.

[9]Rensis Likert, *New Patterns of Management* (New York: McGraw-Hill, 1961); Rensis Likert, *The Human Organization* (New York: McGraw-Hill, 1967).

[10]John R.P. French and Bertram Raven, "The Bases of Social Power" in Dorwin Cartwright and A.F. Zander (Eds.), *Group Dynamics*, 2d ed. (Evanston, IL: Row, Peterson, 1960), pp. 607-623.

[11]Paul B. Malone III, *Love 'Em and Lead 'Em* (Annandale, VA: Synergy Press, 1986), pp. xii-xvii.

THE LEADER SHARES HER PHILOSOPHY

"I AM PLEASED TO BE YOUR LEADER. I'D LIKE TO EXPLAIN MY VIEWS ON GETTING THE JOB DONE AND HOW I OPERATE. FURTHER, I'D LIKE TO DISCUSS MY PRIORITIES, BIASES AND IDIOSYNCRACIES."

PART B

LEADERSHIP STYLES WITH WARTS

Part B, Chapters Three through Twenty, consists of eighteen very short stories, each describing the behavior of a leader in an organizational environment. Each chapter focuses on what I consider a flawed approach to leadership. All of the chapters are a bit unrealistic; I've exaggerated and oversimplified in order to illustrate the style and its effects on subordinates. **Real life is more subtle.** I've tried to provide a variety of settings just to keep your interest and to include both men and women as the "villains". Finally, I've included some attempts at humor in order to make the reading enjoyable. Please forgive me if my "humor" distracts you from the real message–there are leaders "out there" whose characteristics, while perhaps not quite so obvious, are similar to those in the chapters **AND PEOPLE AND ORGANIZATIONS SUFFER AS A CONSEQUENCE.**

Each chapter concludes with four questions, followed by my views of the appropriate responses to each. These responses are based on research, personal experience and discussions with others while teaching military, civilian, blue-collar, white-collar, professional, undergraduate, graduate and executive-level groups. I don't pretend to have all of the answers; I'd be dead by now if I had actually worked for all of these bosses. In fact, I'll be willing to bet that there's no authority alive on **all** of the subjects in Part B. My hope is that Part B will **HELP** you deal with similar leadership situations in the event you ever encounter them and avoid flawed approaches to a terribly significant activity–influencing the behavior of other human beings entrusted to your authority.

CAN YOU SPOT

TESS TERONE

PAM DEMONIUM

SEYMOUR DIGIT

VERNA MATERNA

PHILO PHILANDER

IGNACIO INCOMPETENTI

MINI MINUTIAE

KASSANDRA KAOS

BELLA COSE

YOUR BOSS HERE?

NARDO NARCISSY

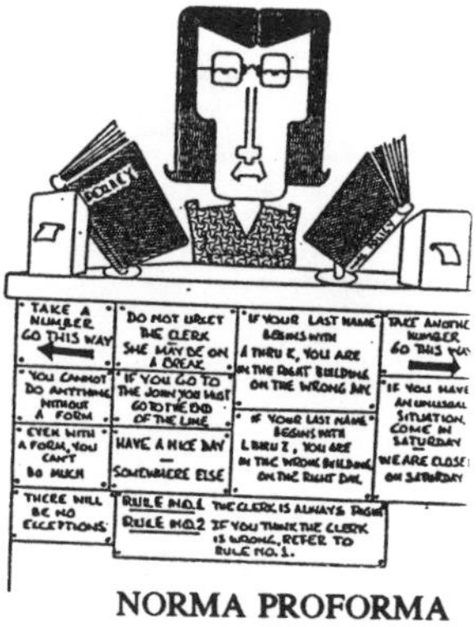

NORMA PROFORMA

RICHARD DEVIUS

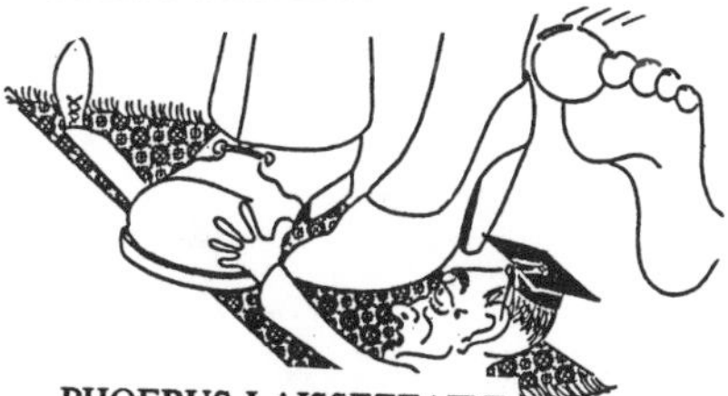

PHOEBUS LAISSEZFAIRE

BURTON BUFFOON

E. STUDLEY STRUMP

ABNER SLACK

AARON ARSHOAL

BLAIR DESPAIR

CHAPTER THREE

TRICK 'EM AND DICK 'EM

"He who governs through deceit and falsehood had better have a marvelous memory." (BIG BOOK, Small Paul to the Phony Baloneys, 33:47)

"Chieftains should never misuse power. Such action causes great friction and leads to rebellion in the tribe or nation."

Attila the Hun[1]

Even in early childhood, Richard Devius had an almost hypnotic or charismatic effect on those about him. People seemed to be attracted to him and were even willing to do his bidding. This contributed to immense satisfactions for Dick. In fact, he took great delight in using people to achieve his own goals–they all seemed so gullible! His first "victims" were his parents who proved to be real suckers when he devised artificial illnesses designed to keep him out of school. Even his older brothers and sisters fell victims to his skillful manipulations. Later, he acquired a "stable" of big, mean followers who took care of his fights in school. Whereas Dick was thin and puny (some referred to him as "sick Dick"), he always "won" disputes with the assistance of his

Abuse 'Em and Lose 'Em

team. Dick usually found a talented girlfriend who did his homework and wrote his papers.

Dick discovered that people responded favorably to praise even when it involved exaggerations and outright lies. He developed a hierarchy of "black lies", "white lies", "quarter truths", "half truths" and "three-quarter truths" and used them as situations dictated. **Of course, he recognized that he needed a tremendous memory to go with this strategy.**

Dick was intrigued by politics. He recognized that people with similar values formed groups, and that these various groups often were in competition. He determined that a clever person could gain great power by manipulating these groups, either in opposition or in combination. **And Dick was a clever person.**

Dick read stories about organized crime and was fascinated by the obligations incurred when Mafia dons did people favors. When possible and convenient, he did favors for others **and stored these favors in his memory bank for future use.**

Very early on, Dick discovered the power of information. Further, he determined that the exclusive possession of certain information could be particularly advantageous. As Dick gained experience dealing with people, he observed something very significant–no one of them was "perfect". It seemed that each had at least one "fatal flaw" in his or her character, or one incident that he or she preferred to forget. Naturally, these people went to great efforts to keep these flaws secret. From then on, Dick tried very hard to identify these "warts" **and record them in his memory bank for future use.**

While Dick took great delight in "beating the system", he recognized that there were risks involved. With this in mind, he developed his "human sacrifice" strategy. If detected in any malfeasance, he was prepared, at all times, to shift the blame to one of his luckless associates. This technique worked beautifully at home with his brothers and sisters, and even with his pet dog, Morris.

Dick was fascinated by spy novels. He discovered the concept of the "cover story" used in espionage. When dealing with deception, it is necessary to develop a "cover story"–a description of what you want people to think. Dick's entire life involved an elaborate series of cover stories. These tested his ability to deal with complexity. **Fortunately for Dick, he had a complex, devious mind and an excellent memory.**

Dick was amused by the quotation, "Do unto others as you would have them do unto you." Naturally, he considered this credo inappropriate for him. At the same time, he realized that the outright violation of the law often involved punishment–even for the very crafty. With these considerations in mind, he determined to live his life in the "gray area" between ethical and illegal behavior, using gullible people with all of their frailties to satisfy his own personal needs. The idea that this would demand extraordinary skills on his part intrigued Dick. **After all, Dick was an extraordinary person!**

After graduation from college, Dick went into sales–primarily securities and real estate. Working right along the borders of illegality, he proved eminently successful. People were so gullible particularly when they were praised and "stroked"! In the process, he did a lot of favors for powerful people. He also collected data on their "warts".

Dick "cashed in" on those favors when he shifted his interests from sales to politics. Those who were reluctant to reciprocate for his favors were reminded of their "warts". In time, they too became Dick's supporters. Dick's years in politics were tumultuous but profitable. He made some mistakes, but was adept at identifying appropriate "human sacrifices" and thus remained relatively "clean".

After a time, Dick pushed his luck too far. His "stable" of "human sacrifices" dwindled; in fact, some of these people started fighting back. Dick even found that he had used up all of his favors and that some people didn't really care about their "warts". He withdrew from politics in middle age and looked for one final opportunity to exert his magical, manipulative powers on gullible people.

Dick discovered that gullible people are most vulnerable when they are dealing with mysterious subjects and where there are significant potential rewards. While he had never been a religious person, he decided that he would be most effective leading gullible people, complete with their "warts" and their need for praise, to the Promised Land. He identified himself as the Grand Magnificence of the Church of What's Happening Tomorrow, developed a spectacular "cover story" concerning recurring dreams and his unique relationship with the Lord, and started providing special favors to his growing congregation.

Unfortunately for Dick, his success as a religious leader was short-lived. During one of his fiery sermons, he fell off the pulpit, hit his head on a collection plate and suffered a concussion. The concussion contributed to a failing memory. Lacking recollections of his "cover story" and his many lies, he was forced to tell the truth. The truth proved to be his undoing. At an emotional church meeting, he was defrocked with considerable enthusiasm, stripped of his Cadillac and theme park, and turned over to the authorities. In desperation, he resorted to a "human sacrifice" defense. Alas, his failing memory let him down again. His "human sacrifice" had passed away several years previously.

WHAT'S GOING ON HERE? WHY IS THIS HAPPENING?

Quite obviously, Dick is a manipulator of people. He relies on their gullibility, vanity, "warts" and stupidity as he abuses power and achieves his own purposes. I suppose there are plenty of Dicks around and that some are even rich and famous. I don't know what their "batting averages" of success are; those who get caught attract a lot of publicity. If you're interested in pursuing the art of manipulation further, I suggest that you read Niccolò Machiavelli's book, *The Prince*, that was written during the Sixteenth Century.[2]

WHAT SHOULD YOU DO IF YOU RECOGNIZE SOME OF THE CHARACTERISTICS OF RICHARD DEVIUS IN YOURSELF?

I'll base my response on practicalities rather than moral issues. It's up to you, but I personally believe that your chances of success become less and less as people become more sophisticated and the flow of information increases. I think there is some kind of "eternal justice" in this world, and that eventually you'll pay dearly for manipulating people. I would hate to base everything I do on lies. My memory isn't that good, and I'd be a nervous wreck. Note that even a powerful nation such as the Soviet Union, **with a system that operated according to state-controlled "truths" (often lies)**, has been forced to change its ways.

WHAT SHOULD YOU DO IF YOU DISCOVER SOME OF THE CHARACTERISTICS OF RICHARD DEVIUS IN YOUR SUBORDINATES?

Warn them once and then get rid of them if they don't change their behavior. I don't think leaders can afford to keep devious subordinates and be associated with liars. The leaders can't afford to believe anything they say. The "stain of deceit" can be cancerous to an organization and ruinous to its leader. People who have been tricked often seek revenge.

WHAT SHOULD YOU DO IF YOU'RE WORKING FOR A BOSS WITH SOME OF THE CHARACTERISTICS OF RICHARD DEVIUS?

If you have any employment alternatives, take them and get out unless you're attracted to organized crime. If you don't have other prospects, operate with extreme caution. Don't accept favors;

don't participate in lies; don't expose your "warts"; cover your flanks and posterior at all times. Be prepared at any time to become a "human sacrifice". With this in mind, document events and keep track of possible witnesses. If your boss's boss is a "straight shooter", consider (1) letting your boss know and then (2) going upstairs to seek help. Whatever you do, recognize that your boss is a manipulator and that he will go to extraordinary efforts to save his own skin. You may be the next to receive the cold steel shaft of treachery.

NOTES

[1]Wess Roberts, *Leadership Secrets of Attila the Hun* (New York: Warner Books, 1985), p. 63.

[2]Niccolò Machiavelli, *The Prince and the Discourses*, Introduction by Max Lerner (New York: The Modern Library, 1940).

If you receive this through the mail, it is possible that someone is telling you something about your style of leadership as perceived by others. Perhaps you should read *Paul Malone's* first book on leadership, **Love 'Em and Lead 'Em** (Synergy Press, 3420 Holly Road, Annandale, VA 22003 — $10.95 plus $1.50 postage).

(FOLD HERE)

FROM: (Optional)

____

____

____

PLACE STAMP HERE

TO: ____

____

____

____

(Staple Here)

CHAPTER FOUR

BUREAUCRATIZE 'EM AND ANESTHETIZE 'EM

"Unfettered bureaucratic behavior can serve itself to the point where there is no reason for its existence." (BIG BOOK, Small Paul to the Perverted Paper Pushers, 49:14)

"Substituting rules for judgment starts a self-defeating cycle, since judgment can only be developed by using it. You end up with an army of people who live by rote rather than reason, and where reason cannot be depended upon."
Dee Hock[1]

Norma Proforma, a veteran of 25 years of employment in a state government, was director of a major department in the governmental apparatus that dispensed state-supported benefits. The department contained over 1,000 employees with offices all over the state. Norma was a precise person. She liked order and certainty; she disliked instability and risk. Part of this was based on her observation of her parents as a child when they owned and operated a family restaurant. Despite extraordinary effort and outrageous hours, her parents eventually failed. Norma was disenchanted by their focus on profit and their unremitting concern

POLICY
MORE POLICY
TAKE A NUMBER GO THIS WAY
DO NOT UPSET THE CLERK SHE MAY BE ON A BREAK
IF YOUR LAST NAME BEGINS WITH A THRU K, YOU ARE IN THE RIGHT BUILDING ON THE WRONG DAY.
TAKE ANOTHER NUMBER GO THIS WAY
YOU CANNOT DO ANYTHING WITHOUT A FORM
IF YOU GO TO THE JOHN, YOU MUST GO TO THE END OF THE LINE
IF YOU HAVE AN UNUSUAL SITUATION, COME IN SATURDAY
WE ARE CLOSED ON SATURDAY
EVEN WITH A FORM, YOU CAN'T DO MUCH
HAVE A NICE DAY — SOMEWHERE ELSE
IF YOUR LAST NAME BEGINS WITH L THRU Z, YOU ARE IN THE WRONG BUILDING ON THE RIGHT DAY.
THERE WILL BE NO EXCEPTIONS
RULE NO. 1 THE CLERK IS ALWAYS RIGHT
RULE NO. 2 IF YOU THINK THE CLERK IS WRONG, REFER TO RULE NO. 1.
D Malone

for demanding and capricious people called "customers". The restaurant venture turned sour due to something called ptomaine poisoning. Norma concluded that such activities were too risky. Upon graduation from college, Norma was attracted to opportunities to serve in the state government bureaucracy. Certain characteristics of bureaucratic organizations appealed to her. First, after a period called probation, the employee became quite secure–a far cry from her parents' experience. Whereas pay in the government was generally less than on the outside, the benefits were good and the retirement plan was excellent. However, what appealed to Norma most was the organization and order. People were specialized and generally knew their jobs. Promotion was based on merit within areas of specialization. There were rules and regulations covering everything. The nagging subject of PROFIT was never discussed since the government provided services and gave away money. Most importantly, the system was designed to be IMPERSONAL with those demanding and capricious persons called "customers" who were dealt with in an IMPERSONAL manner. This seemed to be Norma's "cup of tea".

Norma began employment with the state government in her twenties and worked very hard. Her efforts were rewarded by frequent promotions. She was now in a very prestigious and responsible position. Naturally, all of this satisfied her very much. Her style of management had been a "winner". Let's examine her secrets of success.

As mentioned before, Norma was attracted to order; she hated surprises. Norma determined that the basis of order was predictable performance, and that predictable performance was the result of organizational rules and regulations. Whereas all of the state organizations had their rules and regulations, Norma's always had more–MANY MORE.

Norma experienced frustrations when those capricious and demanding people called "customers" came up with situations (intentionally, she suspected) not covered by her rules. Her reaction was to develop MORE RULES. Her goal was to leave nothing to the judgment of her subordinates–no uncertainty, no surprises. Norma designed forms for every conceivable purpose and form letters to respond to every predictable request. Her policy manuals were voluminous–the pride of the entire state government. In fact, she was forced to develop a policy manual describing how employees should use the other policy manuals. Naturally, all of this took time, and her subordinates had to do a lot of reading–**often while the customer waited.**

Early on, Norma learned the power that goes with making decisions. She reserved this activity to herself; subordinates could refer to the policy manuals–all approved by Norma–for routine "decisions". Norma was frustrated by suggestions from employees who had ideas about doing things differently or "better". She resolved this irritation by creating many levels of hierarchy within her organization and giving her subordinate bosses the authority to say "NO". Only Norma could say "YES". After a while, the nagging problem of unsolicited suggestions virtually disappeared. **Those ideas that survived the "NO BARRIER" took months, even years, to do so.**

Norma relished her professional success and sought evidence to prove her accomplishments. Initially, she encountered problems. She couldn't point to profit since there was none. She had no control over the number of customers served. Finally, she determined that **her proof of "success" would be a function of the size of her organization–the bigger the organization, the more responsibility and authority, the more "success".** With this in mind, she worked her people harder–developing policy, studying subjects hitherto considered unimportant, documenting more than ever–in order to justify more employees. Frequently, this strategy worked, particularly during "good times" when the state coffers were full. However, Norma experienced real challenges when times became tough and the state hired some efficiency experts to "cut the fat" out of the state budget. These very threatening people suggested that, considering the major investment in computer equipment, many of the clerical employees in Norma's organization were actually unnecessary. Norma reacted violently, citing the effect of unemployment, the need for stability, legal issues and the costs of any type of change. She created several study groups to develop massive documents supporting her position. Her ploy worked. The efficiency experts were sent home without ceremony, and their recommendations were soon forgotten. Norma was even able to justify expanding her operation to include spaces for the study groups that became permanent components of the organization.

Despite her personal success, Norma was continually vexed by one population–the capricious and demanding customers. Customers were disorderly and disruptive. Many were actually deceitful in their attempts to obtain state benefits. Many claimed to be "special cases" who should be treated in a special manner–as exceptions to policy. Some even had the nerve to complain in writing to Norma's superiors. In response, Norma developed a series of standard responses appropriate to every conceivable complaint. Further, she came up with a unique "triple filing system" to ensure that every case was properly documented. This resulted in the need for dozens of extra filing cabinets and the justification for additional filing clerks.

Occasionally, particularly irate customers took Norma's department to court. This proved to be a blessing for Norma. She added a team of lawyers to her staff. After all, no bureaucrat worth his or her salt should be without a team of lawyers!

In dealing with customers, Norma determined that each should be treated with suspicion and that "NO" was better than "YES" when dealing with uncertainty. She found that even the most demanding customers tended to give up if delayed long enough. Norma designed her customer service offices as bewildering arrays of elaborate procedures–lines, forms, interviews, approvals, waits and predictable delays to allow for errors to be caught.

Her "front line troops", those who met the customers initially and were under the most pressure, were the least experienced. As employees gained seniority, they earned the privilege of reduced exposure to customers.

Most of Norma's subordinates adapted to the bureaucratic environment and actually mirrored Norma's approach after a short while—a few sought other activities. Since Norma's style focused on IMPERSONALITY, they too left their personalities at home. When dealing with customers, they developed a manner referred to by many as the "stink eye"—a polite but reserved gaze of suspicion totally devoid of emotion. They learned the policies well and applied them without imagination. Those who did this most precisely were promoted to positions with nice offices—away from customers. If they had any new ideas, they stifled them as best they could. While working life could not be considered exciting, it was orderly, secure and comfortable. After all, they could find their excitement bowling or watching X-rated films.

WHAT'S GOING ON HERE? WHY IS THIS HAPPENING?

This could be considered "classic bureaucratic behavior"—perhaps exaggerated a bit but not very much. Bureaucracies are usually large, inflexible organizations that are organized by function and are controlled using elaborate rules and regulations. These regulations frequently provide employees with considerable security. Most employees specialize, and promotions are awarded based on demonstrated merit within areas of specialization. There's an intentional focus on keeping things IMPERSONAL. Further, relative status and position of employees are important. The idea is to provide for predictable behavior through conformance to rigid policies and procedures.

Governmental organizations are often bureaucracies. Unlike businesses that can measure "success" based on profit, "success" in governments is more elusive. This leads to a tendency described in Parkinson's First Law[2]: "Work tends to expand to keep

THE BUREAUCRATIC 'STINK EYE'

"AND HOW CAN I HELP YOU?"

everyone busy." Bureaucracies often allow and even encourage "activity traps", unnecessary work that accomplishes nothing important. With this in mind, it's tough to "kill" an unnecessary part of a bureaucratic structure; it just continues doing unnecessary work and employing people. Sometimes, taxpayers intervene by demanding smaller government. This often results in RIFs—reductions in force, where the most junior (and, therefore, the lowest paid) employees usually "get it in the neck" according to some seniority-oriented policy.

If not carefully controlled, bureaucracies tend to be "inward-oriented". When this happens, people focus on **process** rather than **substance**; **order** rather than **mission accomplishment**. Here is where **the customer, the reason for the bureaucracy's existence**, appears to become an "inconvenience". Of course, this is wrong.

WHAT SHOULD YOU DO IF YOU RECOGNIZE SOME OF THE CHARACTERISTICS OF NORMA PROFORMA IN YOURSELF?

Take a close look at the **mission** of your organization. Recognize that the rules and regulations have a **purpose**, usually the service of some constituency. That constituency or customer must have top priority. Your system must have enough **flexibility** to accommodate individual customer differences and changes in the environment. Develop criteria other than size to measure successful performance; be prepared to eliminate unnecessary (and thus costly) elements of your organization when their existence is no longer justified. Combat your tendencies to be impersonal and overly precise; loosen up; let subordinates use their judgment even if it includes a few mistakes (non-catastrophic). Get out of your office, talk to your people, note how they're dealing with your customers. Encourage suggestions and comments; look for ways to become more effective and efficient.

WHAT SHOULD YOU DO IF YOU DISCOVER SOME OF THE CHARACTERISTICS OF NORMA PROFORMA IN YOUR SUBORDINATES?

Again, make the **mission** and the **customer** your Number One priority. Look for "activity traps" and stamp them out, even if some lose their jobs as a result. Encourage more flexibility in thinking and acting; delegate decision-making authority if subordinates have the capacity. Develop techniques to determine how your customers view your organization.

WHAT SHOULD YOU DO IF YOU'RE WORKING FOR A BOSS WITH SOME OF THE CHARACTERISTICS OF NORMA PROFORMA?

Give him or her what she wants–predictable performance based on the rules. Become an expert in your specialty; work hard; be loyal. At the same time, do your best to ensure that the organization focuses on the **mission** and the **customer**.

NOTES

[1]Tom Peters and Nancy Austin, *A Passion for Excellence* (New York: Random House, 1985), p. 250.

[2]C. Northcote Parkinson, *Parkinson's Law* (Boston: Houghton Mifflin Company, 1957), p. 2.

If you receive this through the mail, it is possible that someone is telling you something about your style of leadership as perceived by others. Perhaps you should read *Paul Malone's* first book on leadership, **Love 'Em and Lead 'Em** (Synergy Press, 3420 Holly Road, Annandale, VA 22003 — $10.95 plus $1.50 postage).

(FOLD HERE)

FROM: (Optional)

____

____

____

PLACE
STAMP
HERE

TO: ____

____

____

____

(Staple Here)

CHAPTER FIVE

BLEED 'EM AND WEEP

"He who covereth his subordinates with manure shall eventually be surrounded by flies only." (BIG BOOK, Small Paul to the People Squeezers, 1:19)

"We have learned how to make man worse. We have acquired knowledge how to control others—how to enslave them, destroy them, dehumanize them."
Peter F. Drucker[1]

From the very beginning, Aaron Arshoal's (be careful how you pronounce Arshoal; it's an old Himalayan family name) perceptions of people were negative. His dad, Alphonse, was something less than inspirational. With an intellect bordering on zombie, Alphonse Arshoal's knuckles barely cleared the ground when he stood erect. However, Alphonse could be mean–really mean. Aaron learned early in life how **fear** served as a motivator. Alphonse's profane tirades sent chills up Aaron's spine and provided techniques that he would use later in life.

Aaron's introduction to the **persuasive power of punishment** came in parochial school. In particular, Aaron admired the performance of Sister Maria Tyrannica, the one with the lead-weighted ruler. While the ruler was used very seldom, its very existence contributed to classroom harmony, psychological submission and complete compliance.

Aaron served for a few years in the Army. His outstanding

performance in basic training was recognized, and he was selected for training as a drill instructor. Part of his new role really turned Aaron on. He thoroughly enjoyed the "initial shock phase" of recruit training wherein new recruits were stripped of all privileges, controlled at all times, and mentally beaten into submission by the military system. However, Aaron became disenchanted with the Army when, later in training, privileges were restored and trainees were encouraged to assume responsibility and develop personal pride in what they were doing. From Aaron's perspective, these "numb-nuts" were incapable of dealing with so much freedom. Aaron declined an opportunity to participate in parachute training. The thought of risking his life using a parachute **packed by someone else** was too much for him. **Clearly, Aaron's view of most people was very pessimistic.**

Aaron completed his military service and turned to civilian pursuits. Initially he was a real estate agent; later he was a stockbroker. In each activity he was a ferocious competitor and made considerable money. However, the roles lacked satisfactions for Aaron. He was frequently required to engage in "unnatural acts"–demonstrating patience and understanding to stupid people who were benefiting from his expertise. Aaron determined that he wanted to do something "big"–something appropriate to his tremendous natural capacity.

Aaron realized that "big" things require organizations; there's just so much a person can do all alone. Inevitably, Aaron must deal with people. He concluded that this could be tolerable as long as he could be the boss.

Aaron did his "homework" and discovered an ideal opportunity to apply his wisdom and energies–a manufacturing plant in a depressed area of a large city. The previous owner had gone "belly up"–declared bankruptcy; Aaron bought the factory for a song. Further, since he was starting operations from scratch, Aaron had the unique opportunity to apply his philosophy of leadership from the very beginning. Whereas Aaron never bothered to share his philosophy with anyone, it could be described

AARON'S VIEW OF AARON

as follows:

1. **People work only because they have to. If work were not required, they would spend their time watching TV, drinking beer and engaging in unsophisticated animal-type activities.**
2. **With very few exceptions, people are stupid. Further, they cannot be trusted. They must be watched constantly or they will goof off or steal from you. Conversely, machines are reliable. They don't get bored, complain or join unions.**
3. **Fear and the risk of punishment are the strongest human motivators. Rewards work sometimes, but too much rewarding spoils people; they expect too much and don't appreciate the reward after a while.**
4. **Society has come up with a lot of laws that limit the power of bosses. While I consider these laws stupid, I will obey them. I'll comply just enough to avoid breaking the law. All that's necessary in order to be ethical is to comply with the law.**

Aaron worked night and day developing his organizational concept. First, he came up with an exhaustive list of organizational rules and regulations–all focusing on what employees **should not** do. These were posted throughout the factory. Next, he analyzed every job in the factory in minute detail. His goal was to "chop up" jobs, thus making each as simple and repetitive as possible–so simple, as Aaron put it, that "any idiot can do it". Wherever possible, he installed machines so that the requirement for employees would be minimal.

It was Aaron's initial goal to ensure that he personally made all decisions in the organization. However, Aaron was forced to admit that this was impractical; some delegating of authority would be necessary. After an exhaustive search, Aaron hired four people–Hugo, Igor, Boris and Bertha–to serve as supervisors. Coincidentally, they appeared to have certain characteristics in common–they were big, mean and menacing. Aaron was careful

AARON'S VIEW OF DESIGNING JOBS

Simple, monotonous, meaningless jobs suitable for blobs.

to delineate their jobs in great detail–they were to enforce the rules, not develop their own.

Aaron's timing was great. Unemployment was high in the area; many people would accept the minimum wage just to have a job. Aaron determined that there was no need for the orientation and training of new employees; the jobs were so simple that virtually anyone could catch on in a few hours. The daily routine was rigid; the rules were specific; Hugo, Igor, Boris and Bertha hovered over the workers throughout each workday. Rules were enforced with ruthless and mindless consistency; there were no discussions or second chances; the slightest infractions of rules resulted in dismissals.

Aaron had no concerns with Equal Employment Opportunity laws. Since he was contemptuous of **all** people regardless of sex, race, color or age, he really couldn't be accused of discriminating–**everyone was treated like dirt.** Since it was assumed that all employees were stupid, training and development programs never became an issue worthy of discussion.

Aaron did have to recognize a few problems that he accepted as "facts of life". First, employee turnover was extraordinarily high. However, since acquiring and training new employees was relatively simple, this didn't bother Aaron much. In fact, the high turnover proved to be a "blessing". With the high turnover, union leaders couldn't find enough workers interested in certifying a union to justify an organizational effort. Next, while the factory consistently met production quotas, the quality of Aaron's products was notoriously poor. In fact, Aaron had to deal with cases of sabotage–intentional acts reducing product quality and disrupting the production process. Finally, Aaron's safety record was so bad that it attracted local area attention. Inexperienced employees, the result of high turnover, were particularly bad safety risks. The simple, repetitive jobs were so boring that employees became careless and suffered injuries. Hugo, Igor, Boris and Bertha were paid for pushing production; safety considerations didn't matter that much. Aaron's annual tax deductions for the state workers' compensation fund skyrocketed as his accident rate exceeded all expectations.

Aaron's initial success proved short-lived. A competitor came out with a higher-quality product at lower cost. The local economy improved, causing the unemployment rate to decline. Here is where the local area image of Aaron's firm proved disastrous. His pool of available workers, available only because of the lack of job alternatives when unemployment was high, disappeared. Since Aaron had demonstrated no loyalty even to his long-term employees, they too disappeared. Aaron was left with Hugo, Igor, Boris and Bertha plus an empty factory. Aaron finally declared bankruptcy, identifying the laziness and stupidity of people as the causes of his demise.

WHAT'S GOING ON HERE? WHY IS THIS HAPPENING?

Aaron's approach to leadership is conditioned by two fundamental factors: (1) his personal arrogance and (2) his pessimistic and contemptuous view of people. This results in a leadership style known as Exploitative Authoritative (Chapter Two) wherein the leader makes all of the decisions and exploits or abuses subordinates. This style worked pretty well in societies dominated by class systems and during the early phases of the Industrial Revolution when most workers were uneducated and living at the basic subsistence level. Many had been conditioned to accept anything in order to make enough money to live. Fear of punishment was, in fact, a very effective motivator. However, as laws and egalitarian trends reduce much of the leader's raw power and people are conditioned to expect more than servitude, there are now many employment alternatives far more appealing than what Aaron offers. Research indicates that there is one particular situation where this style of leadership is still likely to be effective—**short-term, high-priority, crisis situations.**[2]

WHAT SHOULD YOU DO IF YOU RECOGNIZE SOME OF THE CHARACTERISTICS OF AARON ARSHOAL IN YOURSELF?

First off, recognize that many Americans nowadays would refuse to work for you or would quit shortly after being hired. Those who would accept your conditions of employment would not be highly motivated people. There might be some exceptions such as those entering basic military training who expect some "culture shock" and realize that the abusive situation has a purpose and is temporary. Prolonged exposure to this style often results in the "self-fulfilling prophesy"–people who are treated like dolts eventually behave like dolts. If you can adapt, you should consider more optimistic views of people–something closer to Douglas McGregor's Theory Y.[3] This involves taking chances and giving subordinates more freedom and more voice in the decision-making process. If this constitutes an "unnatural act" so far as you are concerned, remain Exploitative Authoritative but be prepared to be limited to the dregs of the American work force.

WHAT SHOULD YOU DO IF YOU DISCOVER SOME OF THE CHARACTERISTICS OF AARON ARSHOAL IN YOUR SUBORDINATES?

It all depends. If you are an Exploitative Authoritative leader, you might want others with similar styles around you. In some cases, even very Participative leaders (Chapter Two) select Authoritative subordinate leaders, relying on the synergistic effects of the contrast (Participative captain of a ship with a very Authoritative executive officer–the "good-guy, bad-guy" combination). However, since there is a lot of evidence that this style is losing appeal, you should consider counseling your subordinates and encouraging them to treat subordinates with greater respect. However, if your subordinates are to change, recognize that they will need "room for error"—some mistakes will inevitably be made as people are granted more freedom. Further, recognize that your subordinates must perceive that changing their styles of leadership will result in rewards they value.

WHAT SHOULD YOU DO IF YOU'RE WORKING FOR A BOSS WITH SOME OF THE CHARACTERISTICS OF AARON ARSHOAL?

Again, it depends. If you don't mind being told what to do and if routine, repetitive work without the requirement to think appeals to you, this might be your "cup of tea". Some people find that working for an Aaron Arshoal, for a short period of time, is a great way to "break into the workplace" and learn a great deal very fast. After exposure to an Aaron Arshoal, subsequent bosses are likely to seem like sweethearts. Further, Aaron Arshoals provide future leaders excellent examples of how **not** to lead. However, prolonged exposure to Arshoal-type leadership can be dangerous. Unexercised brains tend to atrophy. If you have an alternative, my advice is to take it for a short period of time if you must but, by all means, look for something better unless Aaron is in poor health. However, if you have no prospects for alternate employment, give Aaron what he wants—**plenty of productivity**. It is just possible that you can win Aaron's confidence and join the "select" group in Aaron's value system that deserves some freedom and the right to make decisions. Conceivably, **if you can maintain productivity**, Aaron would allow you to use a very different style of leadership with your subordinates. With skill, persistence and a bit of luck, you might do Aaron a big favor—improve his view of most people. The world would improve considerably if many Aarons were to be converted.

NOTES

[1]Peter F. Drucker, *Landmarks of Tomorrow* (New York: Harper & Brothers, 1959), p. 258.

[2]Rensis Likert, *New Patterns of Management* (New York: McGraw-Hill, 1961); Rensis Likert, *The Human Organization* (New York: McGraw-Hill, 1967).

[3]Douglas McGregor, *The Human Side of Enterprise* (New York: McGraw-Hill, Inc., 1960).

If you receive this through the mail, it is possible that someone is telling you something about your style of leadership as perceived by others. Perhaps you should read *Paul Malone's* first book on leadership, **Love 'Em and Lead 'Em** (Synergy Press, 3420 Holly Road, Annandale, VA 22003 — $10.95 plus $1.50 postage).

(FOLD HERE)

FROM: (Optional)

____

____

____

PLACE STAMP HERE

TO: ______________________________

____

____

____

(Staple Here)

CHAPTER SIX

HARASSMENT: NO FUN FOR ANYONE

"He who must use his status in an organization in order to satisfy his erotic needs should consider changing his mouthwash or deodorant or both." (BIG BOOK, Small Paul to the Nocturnal Emitters, 51:91)

"Some people live just to dump on other people. It's almost a form of rape, a sick way to break through the impersonality of a relationship and violate others."
Harvey Mackay[1]

Philo Philander never had much respect for women. The origins of this attitude are obscure. Perhaps it was his embarrassment as a kid when his mother continually referred to him as an "accident" and indicated that she would have preferred another daughter. Or then it could have been the incessant taunting from his seven older sisters and their frequent reference to him as the "runt of the litter". Philo noted that many systems, including governments and religions, seemed to consider women somewhat "inferior". He found this approach "comfortable" noting that even God viewed women as a "side issue"–grabbing one of Adam's ribs to "round things out" in the Garden of Eden. Since Philo wasn't a particularly talented person, it was convenient to classify half of the people of the world less capable than him without further consideration. Philo vowed never to marry. His fulfillment of this

P Malons

vow proved to be no loss whatsoever to womankind.

Philo's disdain for women had absolutely no effect on his sexual appetite. In fact, his preoccupation with sex could be classified as extraordinary. The irony here was the fact that there was something about Philo that seemed to turn women off. This proved extremely frustrating to Philo, whose body seemed to be charged up at all times. For a while, Philo tried obscene phone calls. However, the heavy breathing and whispering gave him a sore throat. He even proved unsuccessful using the 900 "date line" phone systems that cost him lots of money. After very brief discussions, women working on the system developed headaches and hung up abruptly on Philo. While the hookers wouldn't turn Philo away, it was reported that they raised their prices substantially when he appeared.

Philo's frustrations became particularly apparent at work where women were filling an increasing number of jobs. Philo leered, commented, touched when he could–all to no avail. In fact, he was corrected several times for uncontrolled salivating on his work. The crowning blow came when a woman was promoted to become Philo's supervisor. Philo had to swallow his pride and congratulate her. His overture included an "innocent" but firm squeeze where he shouldn't have been squeezing. With amazing speed that seemed to bewilder Philo, he found himself looking for a new job.

Philo's misfortune proved short-lived, however, when a wealthy distant uncle passed away and it was discovered that Philo had been bequeathed ownership of Incorrigible Insurance and Financial Services. Incorrigible was known as the "last chance" provider of the insurance, credit card and financial services industry. In fact, its new Investment Opportunities for the Penniless program had attracted both nationwide attention and police scrutiny. Incorrigible employed 150 people, over half of whom were men.

Philo viewed this favorable turn of events with great glee; his seven sisters contested the will in court. Philo appreciated the fact that his position had automatically made him a wealthy man. However, as much as this pleased him, something else preoccupied his attention—**POWER**. At long last, perhaps Philo could satisfy his primary preoccupation by the "judicious" use of the **POWER** that came with his new position.

Like many others, Philo was subject to fantasies. With the Incorrigible opportunity, one fantasy became an obsession. **At long last, Philo could be preeminent in a domain filled with young, attractive women who were beholden to him for opportunities to earn their daily bread!**

Philo directed all of the energies of his pudgy body toward the goal of making his dream come true. However, he recognized that he had much to do and that he must be cautious. He had heard of "horror stories" relating to sexual harassment and didn't want to be embarrassed by bad publicity—he had to be "cool". Brushing aside the copies of *Hustler* magazine and several X-rated film video tapes on his desk, he developed a "master plan".

His first action was to convince the Personnel Manager of Incorrigible that it was time for him to retire. Philo "sweetened up" his retirement package, accepted his retirement, gave him a crummy watch, and left the position vacant. In essence, Philo made himself the Personnel Manager of Incorrigible and, with that step, became Chairman of Incorrigible's Grievance Committee and Sexual Harassment Committee.

Next, Philo initiated a major restructuring of Incorrigible. In the process, he created several new levels of hierarchy—promotion opportunities for Incorrigible employees. However, he intentionally left these new higher-level jobs vacant; promotions would be decided later based on demonstrated "qualifications" of those who wanted to compete.

Next, Philo took a look at all of the job descriptions in the Incorrigible organization. In the process, he redesigned some jobs, like those in the mail room that required physical strength, to make them more "appealing" to women. Philo noted that no one could possibly accuse him of discriminating against women.

Philo's next initiative involved a close review of his existing work force. He identified employees whom he classified as "losers". While many of them were effective workers, they had certain characteristics in common–they were either men or older women. During the next six months, Philo engaged in a subtle and not-so-subtle program to get them to find other employment.

While all of this was going on, Philo initiated a major recruitment campaign focusing his ads on media read frequently by women. Philo personally supervised the interview and selection processes.

Within a year, the work force at Incorrigible experienced notable changes:

- Eighty percent were women.
- The average age of the employees dropped from 41 to 29.
- The average bra size of the female employees increased.
- The average professional qualifications of the work force declined considerably since many new employees had limited education and virtually no experience.

Philo's dream appeared to be coming true. From the initial interview on, there was a faint but unmistakable message that success in Incorrigible would be influenced profoundly by the enthusiastic personal approval of the President and owner. Further, Philo's glances, smiles and innuendos indicated that he wasn't above a bit of hanky-panky.

Philo engaged in considerable "employee counseling"–all behind closed doors. Promotional opportunities became contests for the "most qualified". Professional travel requirements–Philo always traveled with a group of subordinates–inevitably involved dinner engagements to discuss business and rehearsals of presentations in hotel rooms.

Philo was quick to identify and promote "promising professionals"–all young women. However, demotions and dismissals were equally frequent as, for unknown reasons, the

COMPETITIVE, MERIT-BASED PROMOTION SYSTEM

"Now, Sugar, just work hard and play your cards right and you'll go places in this organization."

"promising professionals" appeared to lose their potential. There were occasional complaints of favoritism and capricious and arbitrary abuse of power, but, as Chairman of both the Grievance and Sexual Harassment committees, Philo was never able to discover any merit in these complaints. Philo was in "hog heaven", at least for a while. Then, everything seemed to "hit the fan".

The case concerning Philo's uncle's will came up in court. It was determined that the will had been written long after his uncle had "lost his marbles". Almost simultaneously, several women employees filed class action suits in court, claiming sexual harassment on the part of Philo and requesting millions of dollars in damages.

WHAT'S GOING ON HERE? WHY IS THIS HAPPENING?

Philo's case is an exaggeration, but there are a lot of men in positions of power who abuse it grossly. Some men feel particularly threatened by a relatively new and very competitive group coming into the workplace—women. Many would like women to return to "traditional roles". Since this isn't possible, some use their power to "fight back" and, in the process, humiliate women. Some see opportunities to use the power that organizations give them to obtain sexual favors. Obviously, their respect for women in general is very questionable. Whereas the statistics vary, surveys indicate that most women in the work force encounter some form of sexual harassment. While sexual harassment roles can be reversed (women harassing men), such occurrences are relatively infrequent. My comments that follow are written in the context of a male boss and a female subordinate.

WHAT SHOULD YOU DO IF YOU RECOGNIZE SOME OF THE CHARACTERISTICS OF PHILO PHILANDER IN YOURSELF?

By all means, change your behavior immediately. Not only are you doing something wrong, but your actions are also illegal. The 1980 Equal Employment Opportunity Commission guidelines state that sexual harassment is a form of sex discrimination. Verbal and physical conduct of a sexual nature is harassment under the following conditions:

- Submission to such conduct is either explicitly or implicitly made a term or condition of an individual's employment.
- Submission to or rejection of such conduct by an individual is used as the basis for employment decisions affecting such individuals.
- Such conduct has the purpose or effect of substantially interfering with an individual's work performance or creating an intimidating, hostile or offensive working environment.

Develop an awareness of behavior that, while perhaps "innocent" in the minds of some men, is viewed as offensive by many women. Recognize that some women, particularly young professionals, are super-sensitive to sexist jokes, terms, remarks, gestures and actions. For example, many are offended by the "fatherly" kisses on the cheek by the male boss when receiving recognition—"would you kiss a man?" Terms such as "Sugar" and "Honey" really turn some women off. If your organization has no policy on sexual harassment, either suggest one or direct that one be prepared, announced, discussed, understood and enforced. Do everything in your power to ensure that one's sex is not considered when selecting, training, promoting or disciplining employees unless there is a legitimate reason to do so.

At the same time, avoid overreacting. Some male bosses avoid

BEWARE OF "INNOCENT" COMMENTS AND GESTURES

"MISS JONES HERE IS A REAL GO-GETTING BROAD. SHE'S WON OUR SALES CONTEST TWO YEARS IN A ROW."

giving women subordinates essential support, counsel and encouragement for fear that their actions might be misinterpreted. That's unfair to the women. Some male bosses have become so fearful of problems with sexual harassment that they "cave in" to any report of problems, even those that have no basis.

WHAT SHOULD YOU DO IF YOU DISCOVER SOME OF THE CHARACTERISTICS OF PHILO PHILANDER IN YOUR SUBORDINATES?

Get tough. Make sure that employees know what sexual harassment is and what procedures are to be followed in the event people are harassed sexually. More importantly, set the example and identify sexual harassment as an absolute "no-no" with severe penalties involved. In some cases, it will be necessary to explain to men why behavior that was "tolerated" in the past is intolerable today. Be prepared for some male resistance, particularly in job fields that were once "for men only".

WHAT SHOULD YOU DO IF YOU'RE WORKING FOR A BOSS WITH SOME OF THE CHARACTERISTICS OF PHILO PHILANDER?

As mentioned previously, this response will be directed to women who encounter sexual harassment from men in the workplace. I will assume that the women reading this do not desire to "play the game" of the harassers. Those women who do run the risk of reputations such as "sleeping their way to the top" and must be prepared for fickle bosses with wandering sexual interests.

First, check to see if the organization has a policy on sexual harassment. If it doesn't, that may be a warning signal. Next, respond to harassment activity, if it arises, firmly and directly. Let the offender know that you're not interested and that you are offended by the remark or action. Record such actions and list the names of possible witnesses–document, document, document. Get performance appraisals in writing, and identify performance goals that are objective (rather than subjective) in nature. Recognize that some male behavior may be "old-fashioned" and actually quite innocent. However, if these activities persist, advise the offender and see your boss. If your boss is the offender, seek help from his boss or the official identified in the Sexual Harassment Policy. I'll stop here due to the complexity of possible subsequent actions such as filing an official complaint or taking the offender to court.[2]

NOTES

[1]Harvey Mackay, *Beware the Naked Man Who Offers You His Shirt* (New York: William Morrow and Company, Inc., 1990), p. 45.

[2]For some excellent additional guidance on this subject, I recommend Lesson 11, "Beware the Office Bully", pp. 45-49, in Harvey Mackay's book referred to above.

If you receive this through the mail, it is possible that someone is telling you something about your style of leadership as perceived by others. Perhaps you should read *Paul Malone's* first book on leadership, **Love 'Em and Lead 'Em** (Synergy Press, 3420 Holly Road, Annandale, VA 22003 — $10.95 plus $1.50 postage).

(FOLD HERE)

FROM: (Optional)

____

____

____

PLACE
STAMP
HERE

TO: ____

____

____

____

(Staple Here)

CHAPTER SEVEN

COMPETENCE COUNTS

"It helps if you know what you're supposed to do". (BIG BOOK, Small Paul to the Incorrigible Misfits, 27:51)

"Hiring today is a more critical process than ever before. A mismatch can cripple a company—and be difficult to get rid of."

James Braham[1]

"That's the wrong grave, Mr. Ambassador; put the wreath on the other grave, sir!" whispered the military attaché as loud as he dared. It was too late. The United States Ambassador placed the wreath in the wrong location at the Independence Day celebration of the emerging nation of Lower Nostalgia while thousands gasped, cameras clicked and flashbulbs flashed. Yesterday's rehearsal in the embassy had been a waste of time; the Ambassador had screwed up again!

Fortunately, the Lower Nostalgians are forgiving people—very unlike the Upper Nostalgians who tend to hold grudges and collect the ears of people they don't care for. The wreath laying ceremony completed, everyone went to the palace for a feast. While there, the United States Ambassador tested his limited fluency in the Lower Nostalgian language with the Prime Minister. This proved to be a mistake since his comment translated into something like "Your mother resembles a frog". Thanks to quick actions by the military attaché, the Ambassador was able to depart early without

Abuse 'Em and Lose 'Em

international incident.

The new United States Ambassador to the independent nation of Lower Nostalgia was Ignacio Incompetenti. Ignacio had made his mark in the world in sewers. He was known as the "sewer king" of the Newark, New Jersey area. In the field of sewer construction Ignacio had no peer; he was good! Indirectly, his work touched many people's lives. He made millions. He decided to contribute large sums of his earnings to a presidential campaign. His candidate won. As a gesture of appreciation, he was appointed the U.S. Ambassador to this emerging nation. Ignacio and his wife, Incontinenta, were ecstatic! Their kids were all married, and the sewer business had become "a drain".

The Incompetentis were invited by the U.S. Department of State to participate in an extensive orientation program in preparation for their new roles. Frankly, they were not very interested in this activity. They rejected the suggestion that they take a crash course in the local language. As Ignacio observed, "American is the international language; we'll get by OK". They were equally unconcerned about courses in Lower Nostalgian history and culture. In fact, they spent most of their time in Washington, D.C. selecting an elaborate wardrobe to wear in their ambassadorial roles. This proved to be somewhat of a mistake since they purchased warm clothing for service in a nation very close to the Equator.

When Ignacio was nominated for the ambassadorial role, the situation in Lower Nostalgia was quite tranquil. The U.S. had no real strategic interests in the area except to support the emergence of a democratic system of government. The Ambassador's initial activities were primarily social in nature. The Incompetentis truly relished this role and attended social functions in the capital almost every night, eating and drinking more than they should. They developed a fondness for the local delicacy, sweet and sour hyena tongue, which was tasty but contributed to severe lower intestinal gas. Within a month, each had put on twenty pounds. Since they were overweight when they arrived, this contributed to problems with their wardrobe, which was far too heavy for the tropical weather of Lower Nostalgia anyway. They continued to eat, drink and sweat. In time, they acquired the nickname in the diplomatic community of "wattacopleashooles", a Lower Nostaligan word that translates loosely as "sweating swine". Meanwhile, the Soviet Ambassador and his wife, while hardly candidates for a beauty pageant, did their diplomatic thing in light, tropical clothing with some expertise.

Ignacio experienced similar problems with his official duties. He irritated the Marine embassy guards by referring to them as "cops". His first news conference in the embassy with the press was conducted with his fly unzipped. He then proceeded to take the members of the press on a tour of the embassy including the super-secret communication and conference room. Before long, his Deputy Chief of Mission, a career diplomat, developed a severe ulcer and had to be evacuated to the United States.

Ignacio's visits to the hinterlands of Lower Nostalgia were equally disenchanting. He insisted on tapping the little children he met on the head–a practice that revolted the local people. He tried throwing coins and condoms at the poor people; no one seemed to appreciate the gesture. On occasion, his limousine returned to the embassy after an excursion, covered with mud and dirtier stuff.

As fate would have it, things changed shortly after the Incompetentis arrived. The Upper Nostalgians, who had been experimenting for some time with Marxism, Leninism, Stalinism, Maoism and Zen Bhuddism, with a smattering of Castroism, were becoming aggressive and were making nasty motions toward Lower Nostalgia. Naturally, the Lower Nostalgians turned to the U.S. for help. Ignacio was excited about a request by the Prime Minister for a meeting concerning how the U.S. might assist in countering this potential enemy. Naturally, he resisted efforts by the embassy staff to help him prepare. The meeting proved to be a disaster. Knowing nothing about defense matters, Ignacio offered SWAT teams, a trainload of mustard gas, an armored division, carrier

"EXPERT DEFENSE ADVICE"

"CHIEF, WHAT YOU NEED IS SOMETHING THAT'LL FOOL THEIR RADAR. NOW, THIS BABY WILL COME IN ON THE DECK AND RIP THEIR KNICKERS OFF . . ."

strike forces and B-52 bombers. For reasons totally beyond Ignacio's comprehension, the meeting terminated abruptly with the Prime Minister putting in a call to the Soviet Embassy.

This situation continued for some time until the sweet and sour hyena tongue finally got to the Incompetentis. They returned to Newark where Ignacio made additional millions in sewers. Meanwhile, in the State Department Control Room in Washington, a light on a huge wall map of the world changed color. It seemed that, without explanation, the nation of Lower Nostalgia had shifted its allegiances from the West to the East.

WHAT'S GOING ON HERE? WHY IS THIS HAPPENING?

Ignacio had no peer when it comes to building sewers. However, as an ambassador, he was incompetent. **Let's face it, we're all incompetent at something!** The problem here is the fact that Ignacio was selected for the job for the wrong reason. This happens a lot. Often highly competent technicians are "rewarded" for outstanding performance by being promoted to supervisory jobs where they are incompetent. This is known as the "Peter Principle"–people tend to get promoted to their levels of incompetence[2].

WHAT SHOULD YOU DO IF YOU RECOGNIZE SOME OF THE CHARACTERISTICS OF IGNACIO INCOMPETENTI IN YOURSELF?

If you have any ego at all, you're likely to live a very uneasy and humiliating life. My advice would be to either (1) take a crash course on becoming competent or (2) request another job that you can do well. The worst thing you could do would be to continue doing your job poorly.

WHAT SHOULD YOU DO IF YOU DISCOVER SOME OF THE CHARACTERISTICS OF IGNACIO INCOMPETENTI IN YOUR SUBORDINATES?

First, try to determine the nature and severity of the problem. Let your subordinates know that all is not well. Then, as in the paragraph above, either (1) help them develop competence or (2) relocate them where they can perform adequately.

WHAT SHOULD YOU DO IF YOU'RE WORKING FOR A BOSS WITH SOME OF THE CHARACTERISTICS OF IGNACIO INCOMPETENTI?

If you're next in line below Ignacio, you might be in a favorable position when his incompetence becomes intolerable. Otherwise, you might spend your life "fixing" his mistakes and being embarrassed by his behavior. There's a hazard to you here. You might become associated with your boss's incompetence in the eyes of others. I'd say you are far better off working for a capable boss.

NOTES

[1]James Braham, "Hiring Mr. Wrong", *Industry Week*, March 7, 1988, p. 31.

[2]Laurence J. Peter and Raymond Hull, *The Peter Principle: Why Things Always Go Wrong* (New York: William Morrow & Co., Inc., 1969).

If you receive this through the mail, it is possible that someone is telling you something about your style of leadership as perceived by others. Perhaps you should read *Paul Malone's* first book on leadership, **Love 'Em and Lead 'Em** (Synergy Press, 3420 Holly Road, Annandale, VA 22003 — $10.95 plus $1.50 postage).

(FOLD HERE)

FROM: (Optional)

____

____

____

PLACE
STAMP
HERE

TO: ____

____

____

____

(Staple Here)

CHAPTER EIGHT

ALL HAIL TO THE CHIEF!

"A firm that rests its laurels on the adulation of one person does indeed skate on thin ice." (BIG BOOK, Small Paul to the Symposium of Slobbering Sycophants, 10:91)

"Seldom are self-centered, conceited and self-admiring chieftains great leaders, but they are great idolizers of themselves."

Attila the Hun[1]

"And that concludes my conceptual guidance for next fall's line", declared Doctor Nardo Narcissy with a flourish as the lights dimmed and a spotlight illuminated his face and body. For a second there was total silence. This was followed by thunderous applause as top-level management of Nardo's Fantastic Fashion Designs rose in unison screaming words such as "sheer genius!", "absolutely magnificent!", "creative beyond belief!", and "author, author!". Nardo Narcissy smiled modestly as the spotlight narrowed to his face only. The group exited the showroom excitedly and rushed to a nearby French restaurant where each member had an opportunity to toast the boss and comment favorably on his creative talents. Nardo accepted each accolade gracefully while occasionally signing autograph books for restaurant patrons who mistook him for a movie star. No one bothered to mention that the line Nardo had just displayed was almost an exact replica of last fall's line except for an idea he had

"borrowed" from a competitor.

Doctor Nardo Narcissy, President of Nardo's Fantastic Fashion Designs, could be considered a "sensitive" person. He needed the approval of others in order to exist. His early life proved very frustrating since approval came infrequently. Then he went into the ladies' fashions business. He was reasonably original, daring and creative with the ability to anticipate trends and "share" the creativity of others when the opportunity presented itself. Nardo's Fantastic Fashion Designs became a big success and very profitable. While Nardo appreciated the profits, he detected the opportunity to gain something even more important—adulation. The people he hired had one common characteristic; they were "natural adulators". Those who lacked these qualities or couldn't develop adulation skills were quickly sent packing.

Nardo had a flair for the dramatic. The executive portions of his office building reflected this propensity. The top floor, Nardo's floor, involved lights, colors and spaces that seemed to "explode" with increasing size and intensity as one walked from the elevators toward Nardo's personal offices. Nardo's likenesses could be seen on walls, partitions and office desks. In fact, all Nardo employees were issued two framed and signed color photos of Nardo; one for the desk, the other for use at home. Nardo buttons and tee shirts were on sale in the lobby on the first floor. A nude statue of Nardo that included the torso of a more muscular man dominated the atrium on the top floor.

Nardo had an unusually large office staff. Just outside his magnificent personal office were three secretaries and two filing clerks, all selected for, among other things, their spectacular personal appearance and their unflagging loyalty to Nardo. This team went through an elaborate "welcoming act" whenever Nardo entered the premises. Further, they went to great efforts to ensure that Nardo saw only the "proper people". Nardo's appointment book was maintained with religious precision. Even when business was slow, people were required to wait to see Nardo just to maintain the illusion of the extraordinary demands on his talents.

As one might guess, Nardo had a limousine with driver; naturally, his license plate read NARDO.

Nardo's personal office resembled a throne room with his elaborate gilt-encrusted desk on an elevated platform and a spectacular view of the city to the rear. Covering the walls were photographs, each including Nardo, that traced every year of his life and highlighted each success. One wall contained nothing but diplomas—everything from his high school diploma to his PhD diploma from the Happy Days Bible School and Correspondence University in California. Naturally, Nardo's office included a massive oak conference table, a wet bar and a bathroom complete with gold faucets and a quilted toilet seat.

In addition to domestic servants in his palatial home, Nardo had a personal staff of two aides—one for domestic activities, one for overseas travel. His Domestic Aide, Ms. Bunny Backside, came from a town in Georgia well-known for the sweetness of its peaches. Among other things (she was a fairly good typist), Bunny had developed an innate ability to fake emotional activities and to praise Nardo's "monumental masculinity" and "skill of a surgeon". However, Bunny was forever suspicious of Nardo's Overseas Aide, Gregory, who had no skills except for wavy blonde hair and a tanned, muscular body. Gregory once commented that he could fake just as well as anybody.

Life at Nardo's was pleasant for those who had no problems "playing the game"—unremitting obeisance to Nardo. Some were better at it than others. Sy Sycophant, a designer relatively low in the hierarchy, disrupted the *status quo* when he presented Nardo with an oil painting of Nardo dressed as a field marshal. Sy was promoted within a week; his unimaginative boss was sent packing.

The organization depended entirely on Nardo making correct decisions since challenging the boss, particularly in front of others, was a "number one no-no". A few were able to manipulate Nardo by making suggestions and then attributing the ideas to Nardo himself. While this involved risks, it was considered to be essential when Nardo, moved by his own "creative genius", became infatuated with ideas that would have destroyed the organization.

While Nardo received consistent approval from members of his organization, some on the outside—particularly competitors and the press—were not always so kind. Open criticism of Nardo from the press inevitably resulted in an explosive, emotional tirade that sent employees scurrying for cover and often resulted in the discharge of the unfortunate person who happened to carry the message. Nardo didn't really mind references to his extreme life style or flexible sexual preferences. However, when critics referred to his work as "uninspired", "pedestrian" or "tawdry", he screamed, sobbed and did terrible things to his gilt-encrusted desk.

After a while, Nardo's staff developed a "standard operating procedure" designed to restore tranquility. Shortly following his initial outbreak, key staff members would enter Nardo's office extolling his virtues and verbally assaulting the offensive critic. Following this ritual, all would proceed to the French restaurant where there were innumerable toasts to Nardo's genius. Finally, Nardo, by then quite drunk, would be taken home by one of his aides—either Bunny Backside or Gregory, depending on his preference at that particular time. Following an evening of faking, the aide would complete the adulation process the next morning with, "Nardo, you're quite an animal!"

Nardo's firm continued successfully until, after a while, his products were generally considered "uninspired", "pedestrian" and "tawdry". Pretty soon, sagging revenues could not support frequent trips to the French restaurant. Key people started turning Nardo's photograph face down on their desks and seeking employment elsewhere. Bunny disappeared with Gregory. Nardo's nude statue was sold to a "way out" nursing home. His "cheering section" dissipating, Nardo could be heard screaming in the "throne room" as his gilt-encrusted desk, now badly shredded, was removed by a team of workmen.

WHAT'S GOING ON HERE? WHY IS THIS HAPPENING?

This is a firm where kissing up to the boss is a vital condition of employment. Everyone has an ego. Some need their egos massaged more than others. Nardo is an extraordinary case. He has the power that goes with being a boss; he uses that power to demand adoration. While most bosses feel that they should receive some "special treatment" because of their status and accomplishments, they don't go to Nardo's extremes.

WHAT SHOULD YOU DO IF YOU RECOGNIZE SOME OF THE CHARACTERISTICS OF NARDO NARCISSY IN YOURSELF?

Recognize that admiration that is **earned** rather than **demanded** is far more satisfying and enduring. Further, realize that "adoring" subordinates are unlikely to provide you "bad news" that would get them in trouble. Draw a line between what "perks" you should rightfully have and those that are frivolous and self-serving. Beware of toadies seeking special favors.

WHAT SHOULD YOU DO IF YOU DISCOVER SOME OF THE CHARACTERISTICS OF NARDO NARCISSY IN YOUR SUBORDINATES?

Discourage such behavior. It contributes to insincerity, lies and hostile people. Further, all of this adulation consumes both time and money. If necessary, give your subordinates some guidance regarding how far they should go in receiving "special treatment". When "special treatment" is appropriate, employees should understand the logic of such policies.

WHAT SHOULD YOU DO IF YOU'RE WORKING FOR A BOSS WITH SOME OF THE CHARACTERISTICS OF NARDO NARCISSY?

If you need the job and your boss is as demanding as Nardo, I guess you'll have to play the "brown-nose game". If this is the case, find out what your boss wants regarding praise and avoid being the bearer of bad news. By all means, don't embarrass your boss, particularly in public. Watch out for competitors who are more adept at "buttering up" to him or her than you are; otherwise you might lose favor. Frankly, I don't care for lying. I'd rather work for someone else even if the pay is less—far less.

NOTES

[1]Wess Roberts, *Leadership Secrets of Attila the Hun* (New York: Warner Books, 1985), p. 102.

If you receive this through the mail, it is possible that someone is telling you something about your style of leadership as perceived by others. Perhaps you should read *Paul Malone's* first book on leadership, **Love 'Em and Lead 'Em** (Synergy Press, 3420 Holly Road, Annandale, VA 22003 — $10.95 plus $1.50 postage).

(FOLD HERE)

FROM: (Optional)

____

____

____

PLACE STAMP HERE

TO: ________________________________

____

____

____

(Staple Here)

CHAPTER NINE

YOUR HUMBLE SERVANT

"Simpering, sniveling and begging doth not a leader make". (BIG BOOK, Small Paul to the Society of the Spineless, 28:77)

"Leadership must be active, not passive; authority must be exercised to be accepted. The strong, distant, placid and silent types idealized in fiction are not the leaders of the real world."

Leonard R. Sayles[1]

"I know that you are all qualified and dedicated professionals", declared Dean Phoebus Laissezfaire uneasily as he looked up from his notes. He realized that this statement was stretching the truth just a bit since some of the faculty were reported to be totally incompetent. He continued, "With this in mind, as your leader I plan to let you do your own thing unencumbered by my interference. However, I will be available at any time to assist you in meeting your personal and professional goals."

The scene was a large classroom at Eastwestern University. Doctor Phoebus Laissezfaire, who had just been announced as the new Dean of the Liberal Arts College, had been introduced to the assembled faculty and was articulating his philosophy of leadership. Some of the faculty present shifted uneasily since they too had been candidates for the position. Professor Passé, well into his seventies, snoozed in a corner unaffected by the distractions of a

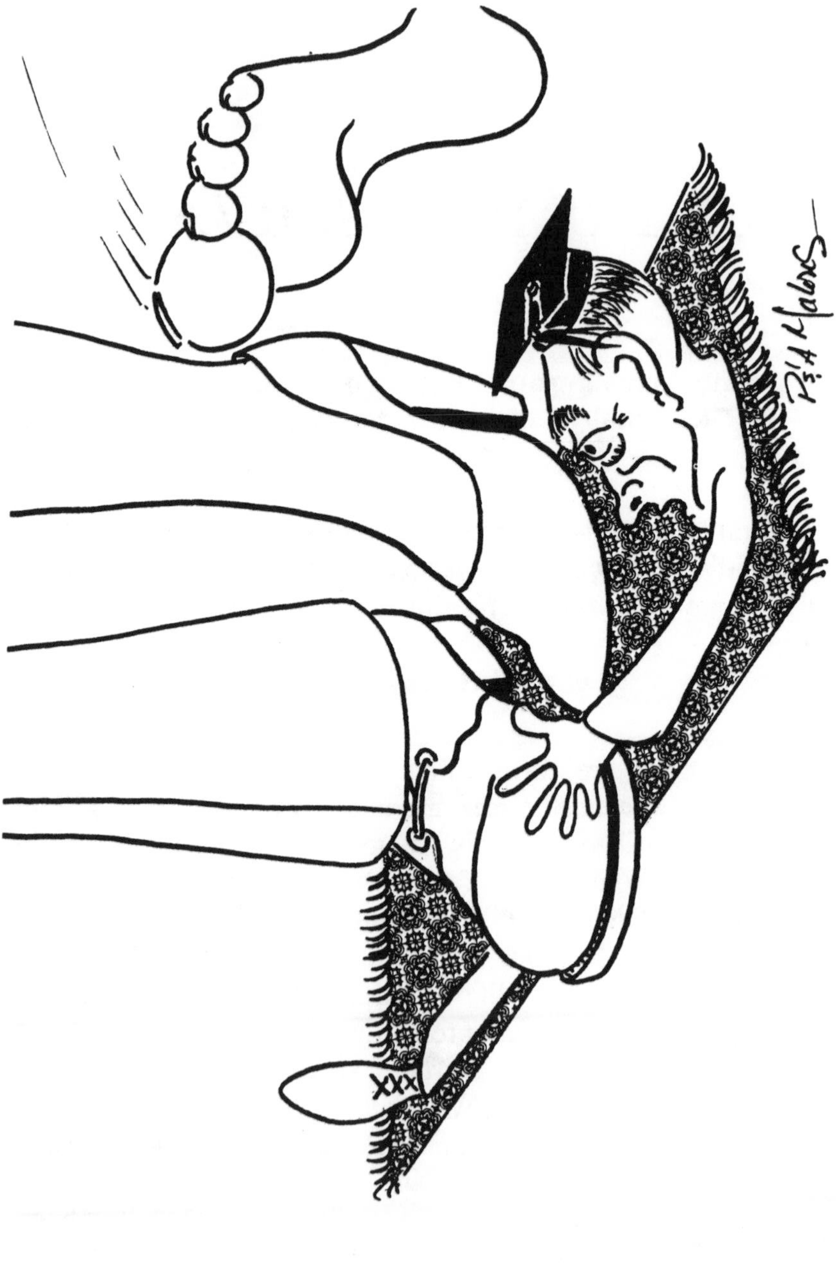
XXX

team from Physical Plant that was replacing fluorescent bulbs in the ceiling in the middle of the classroom. Dean Laissezfaire had considered asking the team to wait until after the faculty meeting, but decided against it. He did not want to make any enemies at this point in his tenure as Dean. His role as leader was to please everyone.

He referred to his notes again and spoke, "I want you to consider us as one big happy family. I am the Dean, but really I'm just one of you ready to serve in any capacity."

Dean Laissezfaire continued for several minutes but sensed that he was losing his audience. Seeking to gain some support, he turned to another page of his script and proceeded, "I am well aware that faculty salaries here at Eastwestern University are well below the national average. You can count on me to fight for adequate remuneration with every fiber of my body!" This statement did attract some attention; even Professor Passé roused; the new Dean had struck a chord of common interest. Pleased with his recovery, the new Dean proceeded to promise spectacular salaries. Little did he know that the University was experiencing a financial crunch and that bleak times were ahead.

Phoebus Laissezfaire was a brilliant scholar, noted for his research and writing in English literature. He had taught at three universities and earned considerable acclaim within his discipline. Seeking some variety in his professional life, he decided to try his hand at academic administration. He scanned some textbooks on management and determined that participative management was "in". Since participative management seemed to coincide with the concept of "academic freedom", he decided to apply the idea in his new role as Dean.

He continued, "I don't pretend to know as much about the University as you. I look to you for advice and guidance. I don't plan to change anything unless you want it that way. The decisions here will be yours; everybody will emerge as a winner! You are the engines of this school; I am but your loyal servant!" He continued with a quotation from Lao-Tzu (565 B.C.):

A leader is best when people barely know he exists.
Not so good when people obey and acclaim him.
Worse when they despise him.
But of a good leader who talks little,
When his work is done, his aim fulfilled,
They will say, 'We did it ourselves'.[2]

He concluded with an inspirational flair suggesting that the assembled faculty sing the University alma mater. The result was disappointing since the pianist had gone out for coffee and no one knew the words to the song. The meeting ended on schedule with Professor Passé asking others what the new Dean had said about faculty salaries.

The Liberal Arts College had been without a full-time Dean for over a year. The interim Dean had been reluctant to take initiatives since his status was temporary. Many unresolved problems and issues awaited the attention of the new leader.

The Dean returned to his office to discover Professor Pontificatus of the Department of Romance Languages waiting for him. The professor, a very senior member of the faculty, began a heated discussion about the sad state of faculty salaries. After a while, it became apparent that his real concern was his own salary. He emoted and fumed and concluded that, "In the name of everything that's fair and reasonable", he deserved a 20 percent increase immediately. Uneasy with the heat of the situation, the Dean agreed and promised to take action. He had won his first friend! However, this decision backfired almost immediately. The Dean discovered that the President of the University personally approved all salary increases. Further, Professor Pontificatus's classes were virtually empty; he had very little to do. He had become an awkward expense for the University. This reversal was a lesson for Phoebus. He had been too "decisive". He would certainly watch that in the future. However, the word had gotten out. The Dean's calendar filled with appointments with other faculty whose eyes sparkled with dollar signs.

Very shortly after the Dean's arrival, the University conducted a convocation ceremony for its graduating students. This ceremony, complete with caps, gowns, the University band, awards and a well-known guest speaker, was a highlight of the academic year. Traditionally, the faculty participated clad in an outlandish array of ceremonial robes and funny flat hats. The President, noting that only three of the Liberal Arts College faculty were present, was furious and bestowed his rage on the luckless Dean Phoebus Laissezfaire.

At the insistence of the President, Phoebus scheduled an extraordinary meeting of the faculty. This irritated most; many failed to attend. Phoebus began the meeting with a comment that THE PRESIDENT was unhappy about faculty attendance at the convocation. He hinted that he wanted to protect the faculty from the ire of THE PRESIDENT. This drew immediate responses such as "Convocations are boring", "My gown needs dry cleaning" and "I don't get paid to dress up and march around." Phoebus defended with a reminder that the Faculty Code included an obligation to attend scheduled ceremonies. This stimulated even more heated reactions such as "Screw the code!" and "You said you were going to leave us alone." What followed was an embarrassing scene where Phoebus begged, offered to arrange for dry cleaning and even pledged transportation for those who needed it. At no time did Phoebus direct the faculty to attend the next convocation. When the time came again, they didn't.

Another issue of considerable importance demanded the Dean's attention. Five years ago, the academic organization that accredited liberal arts colleges had declared Eastwestern's program "totally obsolete" and placed the college on a probationary status. The college Curriculum and Programs Committee had toiled for years to develop a new program better suited to the educational needs of modern young people. For some time, the President of the University had been pressuring the college for a decision. At long last, with a new full-time Dean, there would be action. Or would there?

Phoebus met with the committee. To his dismay, there was disagreement. In fact, there were five separate factions, each fighting for greater prominence in curriculum content. Phoebus tried for consensus–total satisfaction. Not a chance! Then he tried for a majority vote. Even a majority vote was impossible since there were so many options. Phoebus refused to vote since he was "but a servant of the faculty" and didn't want to acquire opponents. After hours of frustrating disagreement, the committee turned to the Dean in desperation, willing to yield to his decision just to free themselves from the continued burdens of committee participation. Phoebus backed off, concluding that the subject "needs further study". The President of the University was furious; the curriculum remains the same to this day; the Liberal Arts College is now unaccredited.

Problems and issues demanding decisions queued on the Dean's calendar at an ever-increasing rate. There was the case of the young Professor Letchh of the Mathematics Department who was reported to be exacting promises of favors from coed students in return for favorable grades. The case was open and shut; it had been investigated and proven that Letchh's grading criteria involved more than numerical dexterity. Phoebus tried to get Letchh's department head to take action, but, according to the Faculty Code, only the Dean had such authority. Reluctantly, the Dean invited Letchh to lunch. After considerable stalling and four glasses of wine, Phoebus mustered the courage to discuss the problem. The result was a prolonged discourse on finite math followed by some fatherly advice that the young professor join an aerobics class and take more cold showers.

Dean Phoebus Laissezfaire soon lost his enthusiasm for academic administration. It seemed that his quest for "win-win" solutions wasn't working. For some reason, every time someone "won", someone else wound up "losing". These "losers" often blamed Phoebus and were no longer his friends. His "bevy of buddies" was diminishing rapidly. Phoebus submitted his resignation and

"I AM BUT YOUR HUMBLE SERVANT.
JUST DO YOUR OWN THING AND WE
WILL BE ONE HAPPY TEAM."

applied for a juicy research project where he could work alone. The President of Eastwestern University accepted the resignation without a blink of an eye. He turned to the resumé of a Dean Brigadier Brutus from a small college who was seeking new challenges in academic administration.

WHAT'S GOING ON HERE? WHY IS THIS HAPPENING?

What we have here is a classic case of a *laissez-faire* style of leadership (Chapter Two) where **the leader assumes a passive rather than an active role.** With a few exceptions, this style doesn't work very well. Most Americans expect outgoing leaders to acknowledge their responsibilities and exercise their authority.

WHAT SHOULD YOU DO IF YOU RECOGNIZE SOME OF THE CHARACTERISTICS OF PHOEBUS LAISSEZFAIRE IN YOURSELF?

If this is your personality and you're getting the results you need, by all means don't change a thing! However, if this isn't the case, you're going to have to become more assertive or find a deputy or assistant who can do it for you. Recognize that not all decisions are "win-win"; almost inevitably someone is going to feel like a "loser". Be prepared to deal with the wrath of the "losers". Further, develop the innards to counsel and, if necessary, punish those who do not play the game according to the rules.

WHAT SHOULD YOU DO IF YOU DISCOVER SOME OF THE CHARACTERISTICS OF PHOEBUS LAISSEZFAIRE IN YOUR SUBORDINATES?

If they have no subordinates of their own, there shouldn't be a problem. However, if they have leadership responsibilities and they can't do their jobs, you should intervene. If you plan to insist that they become more assertive, be sure to back them in their decisions. Some could respond favorably with additional experience or with leadership training that tends to instill confidence. However, some just may not have the "starch" necessary for leadership; they should become followers.

WHAT SHOULD YOU DO IF YOU'RE WORKING FOR A BOSS WITH SOME OF THE CHARACTERISTICS OF PHOEBUS LAISSEZFAIRE?

If you have your boss's confidence and you are an assertive person, possibly you could serve him well by doing his "dirty work"—making his tough decisions for him. However, beware of his vacillating when opposition is encountered. If you have a boss like Phoebus who insists on pleasing everyone, be prepared for extraordinary frustrations, colossal unproductive consumption of time, and an eventual paralysis of the organization as it decays and dies.

NOTES

[1]Leonard R. Sayles, *Leadership: What Effective Managers Really Do . . . and How They Do It* (New York: McGraw-Hill Book Company, 1979), p. 56.

[2]David S. Brown, *Managing the Large Organization* (Mt. Airy, MD: Lomond Books, 1982), p. 235.

If you receive this through the mail, it is possible that someone is telling you something about your style of leadership as perceived by others. Perhaps you should read *Paul Malone's* first book on leadership, **Love 'Em and Lead 'Em** (Synergy Press, 3420 Holly Road, Annandale, VA 22003 — $10.95 plus $1.50 postage).

(FOLD HERE)

FROM: (Optional)

____

____

____

PLACE
STAMP
HERE

TO: ____________________________________

____

____

____

(Staple Here)

CHAPTER TEN

PRESENT YET ABSENT

"He who does nothing should be given nothing to do and be reimbursed accordingly." (Big BOOK, Small Paul to the Living Dead, 71:92)

"You need pride. There are no poor outfits–just poor leaders."

General Bill Creech[1]

"Don't make waves. Do just enough to get by; that's my motto", mumbled Abner Slack as he eyed the clock and continued to brief his successor as Chief of the Department of Non-Controversial Administrative Support in a large Federal Government agency. Dora Doright, who was taking notes, reacted in disbelief, but Abner was apparently serious–dead serious. He eyed with obvious disinterest a stack of approximately forty telephone notes on his otherwise clean desk. Abner was preparing to retire in a month after thirty years of government service; Dora was to be his successor. Actually, Abner had "retired" five years ago. Since then, he had put in time with full pay and allowances. The only people who suffered were his immediate subordinates, the agency he worked for and the American taxpayers.

Abner did not begin his professional life with this attitude. In fact, he entered Federal Government service with great enthusiasm.

DO NOT
DISTURB

He found the work to be interesting and reasonably challenging. More importantly, he appreciated the opportunity to serve the country he cared for very much. Further, he was aware that the Federal Government served as a "laboratory" for social change in the country. Many initiatives regarding the provision of opportunities for minorities and women were tested first within the Federal Government.

Abner applied himself with considerable zeal; his work was recognized by frequent promotions, highly visible positions and the distinction of his being recognized as a "star" in his organization. He developed an ambitious career plan that included rising to the top of the Civil Service ladder.

For the first twenty years, Abner's plan was "on track". Then, things began to change. He had some health problems and then went through a nasty divorce. He began to drink, occasionally to excess. He missed a promotion that he thought was a "sure thing"; instead, a younger female worker got it. For the first time in his life, the annual appraisal of his work performance contained critical comment–from the same woman! Abner felt betrayed by the system he had served so very well. He determined that he could not afford to retire. Instead, he decided to "retire unofficially".

Abner's department contained 150 employees engaged in routine, labor-intensive, administrative jobs. While not highly visible, the department provided essential services to the agency it supported. Abner determined precisely how little the department could accomplish without his getting into trouble–and aimed at this minimum. Sour on people in general–people had contributed to his demise–he decided to ignore them as best he could. He developed a philosophy of leadership best described as "Be present, but Absent." Abner "absented" himself in an office behind a door that was almost always closed except when he went to and from work and lunch. He even had a private bathroom installed to avoid "unnecessary exposure" to his subordinates.

Abner was a great delegator. He farmed out all tasks to subordinates with this advice: "Don't take chances; don't get me into trouble; don't change anything; don't bother me unless it's absolutely necessary." When Abner's subordinates made mistakes attracting attention, he was quick to disavow any responsibility and left them "high and dry". At no time did his guidance include any references to "quality work", "improving performance" or "ethical behavior".

Abner went to extraordinary efforts to avoid people. His was the only department in the agency that never had an annual Christmas party. He often sent his deputy to meetings with his own boss, citing illness or conflicting obligations. Meetings with his own subordinates were infrequent and brief. With the exception of a very few people, he knew none of his subordinates' names. In fact, when he was required to submit annual appraisals of subordinates' performance, he was often unsure of whom he was rating. Actually, it didn't make much difference since all were rated about the same–a low average. Problem employees were tolerated; outstanding employees were generally ignored. He made it very clear that employees must leave their personal problems at home and that he was totally unavailable to counsel those needing help.

The impact of Abner's leadership style could be categorized in one word–LETHARGY. Bare minimums were usually achieved. Often, backlogs occurred; eventually they were resolved if there was pressure from higher up. Employees "went through the motions" totally unconcerned and bored. Nothing ever changed unless change was demanded from higher up. When this happened, the change was painfully slow. Morale was generally poor. Absenteeism was high. Prolonged absences of employees–coffee and lunch breaks–were common. Smokers (smoking was not allowed in the building) were known to require at least twenty minutes to satisfy their tobacco needs–and no one really cared. There were no awards for outstanding performance since there wasn't any. There were never any official visitors; the agency directed guests to other offices that weren't "embarrassments".

SOME "STARS" LOSE THEIR SHINE

Abner sat in his office watching the clock tick slowly toward quitting time. Dora Doright had departed, her orientation of twenty minutes completed. Abner mused, "I'll certainly be glad to retire and relax." He had a point. While he was doing virtually no work, it was difficult to relax. He knew that someone could blow the whistle on him at any time. Abner's secretary buzzed to advise him that the agency head was on the telephone. "Tell him I'm not in", responded Abner. Abner's secretary lied; she had lots of practice at that. True to form, Abner was "Present but Absent".

WHAT'S GOING ON HERE? WHY IS THIS HAPPENING?

What we have here is a style of leadership classified as "impoverished".[2] You might recall the leader's "balancing act" in Chapter Two. Leaders balance the needs of the organization and the needs of the subordinates. In Abner's case, he doesn't care about either. Abner has withdrawn from the obligations of leadership while continuing to accept full pay and allowances. In my opinion, this is unethical and certainly unfortunate for the organization and Abner's subordinates. Note that Abner had previously been a "hard charger". Some people, particularly those in mid-life, suffer personal setbacks or experience "burnout" (extraordinary stress and a loss of satisfaction of rewards that were once important)[3] and resort to this type of behavior. You might find quite a few Abners lurking in inconspicuous places, particularly in large organizations.

WHAT SHOULD YOU DO IF YOU RECOGNIZE SOME OF THE CHARACTERISTICS OF ABNER SLACK IN YOURSELF?

If you detect "Abner tendencies" in yourself, you're probably not a very happy person unless you've been this way all your life. Perhaps what you need is a refreshing change of pace, possibly a vacation, to get your "vital body juices" rejuvenated. If the problem is more profound, it is possible that you need a major change in your life. Note the diagram on page 112 of the "typical" single career that uses "success" as a dimension. You may be in the decline phase–not much fun after years of success. Now look at an alternative view–multiple careers with "personal satisfaction" as the critical dimension. If you're eligible for some form of retirement (and a degree of financial security), why not consider finding out what you really want to do and embarking on another "career"? If this isn't possible, force yourself to change your behavior and give both the organization and your subordinates what they rightfully deserve.

WHAT SHOULD YOU DO IF YOU DISCOVER SOME OF THE CHARACTERISTICS OF ABNER SLACK IN YOUR SUBORDINATES?

A lot depends on their past histories. If they're relatively new to the organization, you don't "owe" them much–they might be candidates for warning followed by possible discharge. However, if your Abners have served the organization well in the past, your obligations increase. In my opinion, you owe it to them to (1) help determine the nature of the problems and (2) offer opportunities for them to seek assistance in resolving their problems. Note that I view Abner's behavior as unacceptable; Abner must change or you, his leader, must take decisive action. What should you do; how far should you go? Again, it depends. Obviously, the "ultimate action" is discharge. However, some organizations avoid this action and "hide" their Abners in inconspicuous places until they're eligible for retirement. If you're going to do this, by all means don't give Abner any subordinates; he might "contaminate" them.

TRADITIONAL CAREER PATTERN

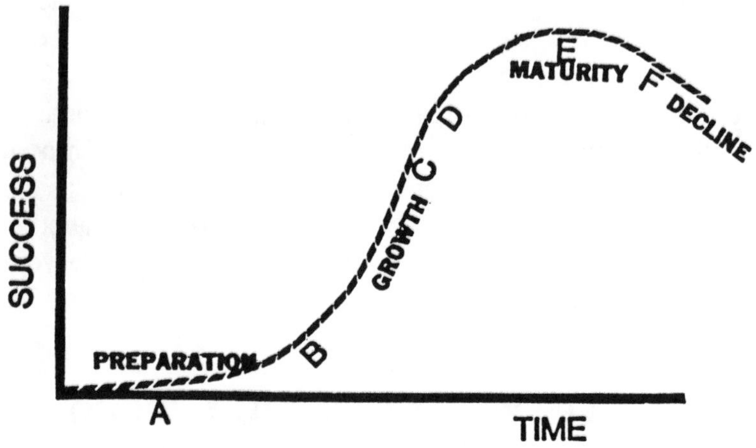

PROPOSED CAREERS PATTERN

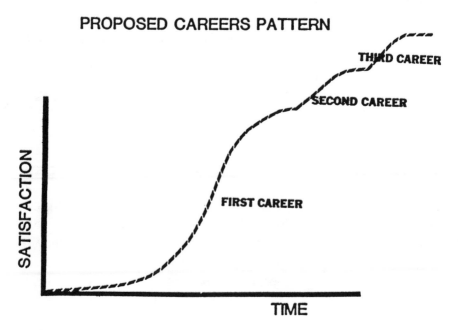

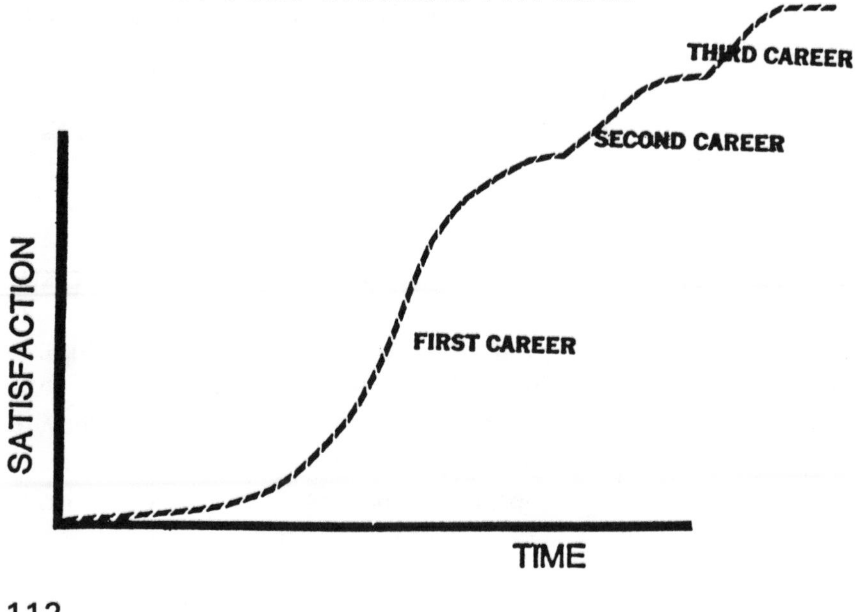

WHAT SHOULD YOU DO IF YOU'RE WORKING FOR A BOSS WITH SOME OF THE CHARACTERISTICS OF ABNER SLACK?

In my opinion, you're in a very undesirable position unless Abner is on the way out. If that's the case, you can emerge as a "star" when Abner leaves–almost any leadership style will be an improvement. However, if Abner is scheduled to stay, I suggest that you seek employment elsewhere–virtually anywhere. Abner's indifference can be contagious. Abner's typical "low average" performance ratings can hurt your career potential–you can be "killed by faint praise". Finally, you will be associated with Abner, a real "loser". That association could "taint" your entire professional career.

NOTES

[1]Tom Peters and Nancy Austin, *A Passion for Excellence* (New York: Random House, 1985), p. 238.

[2]Robert R. Blake and Jane Srygley Mouton, *The New Managerial Grid* (Houston: Gulf Publishing Company, 1978), p. 11.

[3]C. Maslach and S. E. Gackson, "Burned-Out Cops and Their Families", *Psychology Today*, May 1979, pp. 59-67.

If you receive this through the mail, it is possible that someone is telling you something about your style of leadership as perceived by others. Perhaps you should read *Paul Malone's* first book on leadership, **Love 'Em and Lead 'Em** (Synergy Press, 3420 Holly Road, Annandale, VA 22003 — $10.95 plus $1.50 postage).

(FOLD HERE)

FROM: (Optional)

____

____

____

PLACE
STAMP
HERE

TO: ______________________________

____

____

____

(Staple Here)

CHAPTER ELEVEN

TANTRUM TYRANNY

"He who governs through fits of rage soon becomes outrageous." (BIG BOOK, Small Paul to the Benevolent Order of Tranquility Tramplers, 72:51)

". . . you do not lead by hitting people over the head. Any damn fool can do that, but it's usually called 'assault' and not 'leadership'."

General Dwight Eisenhower[1]

Bella Cose was brought up in a large family. Whereas there was considerable love in this family, there was also continual discord. Jammed into a small apartment with limited facilities in a very large city, members of the Cose family had to struggle in order to be heard and get their "piece of the pie". It seemed that noise was a way of life, and that the noisiest won the battles. Cose family disagreements could be monitored a block from the apartment. Occasionally, the police were called by neighbors when the volume and the emotion level seemed threatening.

Bella was a sensitive and emotional girl in school. Once again, she observed that the meanest, most aggressive and most assertive

Abuse 'Em and Lose 'Em

kids seemed to get more than their share of the "goodies". In many cases, they even intimidated the teachers. On the street, Bella witnessed the hostility, rancor and verbal abuse that many employed when relating to other people in their daily lives. All of this contributed to her frustrations and anger, which she let out in the family apartment when seeking her "piece of the pie".

Bella was a particularly driven person. Determined to be successful in professional life and achieve what her parents hadn't, she applied all of her energies to her work. In the process, she developed hypertension and an acid stomach that required frequent medication. While she was a temperamental person, she confined her frequent emotional outbursts to her husband and activities away from the office.

After ten years, Bella's efforts in her firm were recognized in the form of a promotion to the position of branch chief in an office with 20 employees. Naturally, this recognition was very satisfying to Bella; at long last she was going to have some control over her life. Further, Bella decided that, along with the responsibility that went with the job, she had earned the right to be herself without the frustrations associated with holding back her emotions. Recalling her earlier life, she concluded that people do respond to emotional outbursts. Since her job now included getting others to work, she could put her pent-up emotions to productive use.

What followed for over a year was an office environment characterized by observers as "management by tirade". Bella's "style" involved periods of serenity punctuated by totally unpredictable explosions of violent anger and hostility. As time went by, the explosions became more frequent; Bella had become a walking time bonb. Bella's subordinates, who knew her as a quiet, hard-working employee, were taken completely by surprise.

As the realities of Bella's leadership style began to sink in, employees adapted. The primary tactic was avoidance, although this was difficult in a confined office space. It was determined that Bella was always in a "snit" when she arrived at work after driving from the suburbs and trying to find a parking space. The first

"FELLA, HAVE YOU GOT A MATCH? LIGHT MY FIRE AND MAKE MY DAY!"

employee she spotted, regardless of guilt or innocence, inevitably received blistering criticism in a voice that could be heard in the first-floor lobby. Apprehensive subordinates maneuvered carefully to avoid being the first to be seen by Bella, but someone had to receive the "Bella Breakfast Blast". What followed included many tearful scenes and a few resignations. However, jobs were scarce and most stayed and adapted.

Since Bella's outbursts could be caused by virtually any situation, the quality of the work in the office did not improve; no one was quite sure how to please the boss. Employees measured "success" based on avoiding the tirade rather than achieving excellence. Defensive and apprehensive themselves, they bickered frequently and used every day of their sick leave. Office "high points" became periods when Bella went on vacation or was engaged in business travel. Bella's "mood of the day" appeared to be the most significant topic of office conversation.

Bella's behavior could not be ignored by higher-level management–the organizational grapevine was full of "Bella stories", many exaggerated but scary enough to attract attention. After two counseling sessions that left Bella in tears–and resulted in blistering episodes with her subordinates–Bella was reassigned to a special assistant position where she had only one subordinate, a handicapped man who was totally deaf.

WHAT'S GOING ON HERE? WHY IS THIS HAPPENING?

Everyone in life experiences frustrations and tensions–some more than others. Some react to stress impassively; others show their emotions through their behavior. In this case, Bella has taken advantage of her power as a leader to vent her emotions on luckless and innocent subordinates. Sparring partners are paid to serve as punching bags; most employees are not. This is an abuse of power and totally unfair. Further, it contributes to subordinates who are "failure avoiders" (avoiding the blistering emotional outbursts) rather than "success seekers" (committing themselves to high-quality work).

WHAT SHOULD YOU DO IF YOU RECOGNIZE SOME OF THE CHARACTERISTICS OF BELLA COSE IN YOURSELF?

If your behavior is as extreme as Bella's, you probably should visit a psychiatrist. If you tend to enjoy berating and humiliating subordinates, you have become a bully. Bullies should not be entrusted with the responsibility of influencing the lives of other human beings. While occasional outbursts of emotion can be justified and may achieve desirable results, no one benefits from a "steady tantrum diet". Remember that your judgment is not at its best when you are highly emotional. By all means, try to find some more socially acceptable and humane way of venting your emotions. Some Japanese firms even go so far as to provide punching bags with faces of top management officials for subordinates to pound on when they're frustrated.

WHAT SHOULD YOU DO IF YOU DISCOVER SOME OF THE CHARACTERISTICS OF BELLA COSE IN YOUR SUBORDINATES?

As mentioned above, you're dealing with an intolerable situation if the behavior is as extreme as Bella's. I believe that you, as the leader, should counsel the subordinates, try to find the causes, and take actions to change the situation. Many organizations have Employee Assistance Programs that provide confidential, low- or no-cost, expert assistance in dealing with employee personal problems. If all appropriate efforts fail, move the individuals to non-supervisory positions where subordinates are not required to be bullied by abusive bosses in order to earn their daily bread.

WHAT SHOULD YOU DO IF YOU'RE WORKING FOR A BOSS WITH SOME OF THE CHARACTERISTICS OF BELLA COSE?

Unless you're some sort of masochist, it's not likely that working for someone like Bella would be fun. Recognizing this, the question of available alternative employment comes up. Some people can endure bullying better than others. In fact, some can virtually ignore the verbal abuse ("it's just part of the job—nothing personal"), develop effective avoidance techniques, or even, in some cases, fight back. Personally, I'd look for another job if it looks like Bella isn't going to change and will survive for some time.

NOTES

[1]David S. Brown, *Managing the Large Organization* (Mt. Airy, MD: Lomond Books, 1982), p. 228.

If you receive this through the mail, it is possible that someone is telling you something about your style of leadership as perceived by others. Perhaps you should read *Paul Malone's* first book on leadership, **Love 'Em and Lead 'Em** (Synergy Press, 3420 Holly Road, Annandale, VA 22003 — $10.95 plus $1.50 postage).

(FOLD HERE)

FROM: (Optional)

____

____

____

PLACE
STAMP
HERE

TO: ____

____

____

____

(Staple Here)

CHAPTER TWELVE

EVERYTHING IN ITS PLACE

"Discrimination is a necessary element of decision-making. Be sure your criteria are appropriate and fair." (BIG BOOK: Small Paul to the Snob Hill Society, 3:51)

"The 'Old Boy Network' is elitist; the new network is egalitarian."
John Naisbitt[1]

E. Studley Strump had strong views concerning social order. He believed that some people with certain characteristics had basic rights to live particularly rewarding lives–palatial homes, luxurious life styles, many servants, attendance at the right schools. Then, according to E. Studley's "social order", others should have opportunities to "fill in" and serve in lesser positions–reduced rewards and satisfactions. Of course, certain other groups must operate near the bottom and do the "dirty work" necessary to keep the system going. With this "natural harmony", the engines of progress should, in E. Studley's view, proceed in an orderly manner.

E. Studley attended a prestigious northeastern university and immediately went to work for his father in the massive Humongous Industries, a conglomerate with billions of dollars in annual revenues. E. Studley served the organization well and was

P Malous

eventually selected as President.

Almost immediately, E. Studley received an opportunity to apply his "social order" theory in the workplace. Planning was in progress for the relocation of the corporate headquarters to a new skyscraper in New York. Planners were in the process of designing office spaces and determining who goes where. Their strategy had been to put people together according to the existing flow of work. E. Studley changed that. He provided the following guidance: "Office spaces and related activities will be assigned according to the person's level in the Humongous hierarchy. Height equates to achievement; the higher one's position, the higher he is in the building. Naturally, I will occupy the top floor. My executive vice presidents will be on the floor below, ordinary vice presidents on floors below them and so on. Naturally, those in executive positions will have their own eating facilities and parking lots and use a separate elevator system."

After that, E. Studley went into considerably more detail. Status in the organization determined the size of offices, the number of windows, the thickness of rugs, the location of parking facilities, the access to toilet facilities–even the quality of the solid wood or veneer of the desks.

Physical arrangements to his satisfaction, E. Studley then turned to his work force–his people. He realized that he would have to be subtle in this effort since Equal Employment Opportunity laws tended to disrupt his view of the natural "social order".

First, E. Studley turned to his executive-level subordinates. As they dined in elegant splendor in the Executive Dining Room overlooking the masses in the streets below, he reminded them that they were "special", a team with special views and values. He encouraged them to live up to this responsibility, to wear special clothes, to drive special cars, to join special country clubs, to marry, have children and send them to special schools, to vote for the right people–just like he did. At the time of his talk, E. Studley happened to be wearing a blue, pinstriped suit and a red tie. Within a week, all in the Executive Dining Room happened to be wearing the same ensemble. In fact, blue, pinstriped suits with red ties became the "uniform" for Humongous executives—all others in the organization were strongly discouraged from wearing such attire. As time went by, the word got out that gray was the proper color for those in suits below a certain floor in the headquarters building. Floors 13 to 22 immediately became known as the "gray zone".

E. Studley then turned his attention to the remainder of the Humongous work force. He spent many hours with the Vice President for Human Resources, discussing his views of "appropriate people" and "acceptable behavior". E. Studley made it perfectly clear that there would be a certain degree of "social order" within Humongous with very distinct "hierarchial barriers" erected at various levels. People would be permitted to cross these barriers only with the personal approval of E. Studley Strump. Satisfied that the seeds of his "social order" approach had been sown, E. Studley then turned to the business of making profits. The seeds took a while to germinate fully, but germinate they did.

Not surprisingly, the executive-level group at Humongous developed consistent characteristics. They were all tall, white males of Protestant faiths who had many children. As time went by, most took up golf; E. Studley happened to play golf. When E. Studley complained about the effects of the trade imbalance on the economy and business in general, all traded in their Mercedes, Toyota, BMW and Volvo cars for luxury American vehicles. They were a very harmonious group both at work and at the fashionable country club most belonged to.

When one descended below the 23rd floor at Humongous, significant changes could be detected. Most apparent, a few women were in positions of responsibility. There were managers with Jewish names and people of Irish, Polish and Italian heritage—even Catholics. They wore their gray suits daily with consistent fidelity and rarely spoke of climbing above the 22nd floor.

Descent to the 12th floor and below, where the "dirty work" of the Humongous headquarters was done, revealed even greater variety with black, Hispanic, Asian and other groups—all heterosexual. These employees wore anything they wanted unless they were very ambitious—those wore gray.

On occasion, Humongous encountered bad publicity in the form of charges of "discrimination". Anticipating this, E. Studley personally approved a select few "barrier crossers", as they were known. One of these was a tall, white, Protestant woman who was promoted to a Vice President position with considerable publicity. This woman was assigned very insignificant responsibilities but was displayed prominently for all of the world to see. In time, she took up golf, sold her Honda and blended into the executive team. She thought that perhaps her success would contribute to profound changes at Humongous, but, no, E. Studley Strump remained committed to his concept of "social order" until one fateful day when he was struck by lightning on the golf course.

WHAT'S GOING ON HERE? WHY IS THIS HAPPENING?

This is an application of the traditional class system—very commom in societies of the past but now declared both immoral and illegal in the United States. However, bad habits are tough to change. There are some who cling to the old "social order" thinking and do their best to preserve it. While many of the obvious barriers to the historical "outs" of society have been reduced, some more subtle techniques exist and persist. Note that the "social order" approach also involves a focus on harmony and conformity—"acceptable" behavior and dress of various social groups.

WHAT SHOULD YOU DO IF YOU RECOGNIZE SOME OF THE CHARACTERISTICS OF E. STUDLEY STRUMP IN YOURSELF?

First off, convince yourself that what you're doing is not only illegal; it's immoral. If you can't do that, you'll spend your life "going through the motions" of Equal Employment Opportunity. Next, with regard to all employment considerations, look at each person as an **individual**, not as a member of any particular group of people (men-women, old-young, black-white, etc.). By all means, avoid stereotyping groups of people if you can. Further, don't require that your subordinates become "cookie-cutter cutouts" of you; allow them some freedom with regard to their beliefs and their behavior. Limit your requirements for conformity to those things that are **essential** for the organization to accomplish its mission.

COMMENT:

Leadership, a "fine art", always involves human judgments. Some leaders, reacting to discriminatory abuses of the past, give the previous "outs" special opportunities. That's what Affirmative Action is all about. Some go too far and eliminate all opportunities for advancement for the previous "ins" (in most cases, white men). This too can be grossly unfair.

WHAT SHOULD YOU DO IF YOU DISCOVER SOME OF THE CHARACTERISTICS OF E. STUDLEY STRUMP IN YOUR SUBORDINATES?

Attack the problem on both a moral and a legal basis. If the moral case isn't persuasive to your subordinates–attitudes can be tough to change–focus on the legal issue and the need for fairness. Try to explain WHY the subject is important and that the barriers used by traditional discriminatory systems are artificial barriers. You may have to prove your case and demonstrate that some of the "outs" can really produce. Remember that some are threatened when they are forced to compete equally with greater numbers of people. For example, white men, the traditional "ins", must now compete equally with far more people than in the past.

WHAT SHOULD YOU DO IF YOU'RE WORKING FOR A BOSS WITH SOME OF THE CHARACTERISTICS OF E. STUDLEY STRUMP?

Be prepared for some decisions that are grossly unfair. Depending on your status, you might benefit or lose. Eventually, someone is going to "blow the whistle" on Studley. The result of this could be major damages and organizational chaos as the mistakes of the past are rectified. I'd say that, unless you have an opportunity to change the system and make it better, you should work elsewhere.

NOTES

[1]John Naisbitt, *Megatrends* (New York: Warner Books, Inc., 1982), p. 197.

If you receive this through the mail, it is possible that someone is telling you something about your style of leadership as perceived by others. Perhaps you should read *Paul Malone's* first book on leadership, **Love 'Em and Lead 'Em** (Synergy Press, 3420 Holly Road, Annandale, VA 22003 — $10.95 plus $1.50 postage).

(FOLD HERE)

FROM: (Optional)

____

____

____

PLACE
STAMP
HERE

TO: ____

____

____

____

(Staple Here)

CHAPTER THIRTEEN

NO JOKING MATTER

"He who follows a horse's ass too close for too long develops nasal congestion, blurred vision and an acid stomach." (BIG BOOK, Small Paul to the Distinguished Order of Ding-a-Lings, 59:11)

"One who appears as a jester of the courts will receive deference as the same."
Attila the Hun[1]

From the very first day he was born, there was something special about Burton Buffoon–he made people laugh. Whereas most babies are cute and get lots of "oohs", "ahs" and smiles, Burton's antics, even as an infant, had people rolling in the aisles. Tiny Burton was no fool; he liked ATTENTION; he kept it up.

Throughout his school years, Burton was known as the class clown. He loved ATTENTION and went to great lengths to get it. He made strange noises, wore unusual clothing, engaged in outlandish behavior–all while his classmates roared their approval. As he was promoted from grade to grade, his screams for ATTENTION became more sophisticated–even stranger and louder noises, water balloons, whoopee cushions, mimicking teachers, practical jokes on one and all. While he hurt a few feelings and

Abuse 'Em and Lose 'Em

won few friends among the teachers, he got what he really wanted—ATTENTION.

College was a breeze for Burton who was a good student. More importantly, he was beyond the controls of his parents who tended to inhibit his more extreme behavior. He was free to express his creativity and ATTRACT THE ATTENTION OF GREATER NUMBERS OF PEOPLE. He joined the Beta Beta Beta fraternity and eventually became its program chairman. After a year in this position, the university terminated the fraternity charter, and no sororities would participate in Beta Beta Beta parties. Burton considered these events hilarious since he was ready to graduate anyway. Beta Beta Beta's Bacchanalian Orgy, a product of Burton's fertile mind, had been a social event few in the university would ever forget. He framed the photo of him being led to the police cruiser by the security guards.

Still seeking ATTENTION, Burton decided to be an actor. However, he discovered that the dramatic arts weren't quite ready for his style. He then reexamined the job market and decided to try his hand at advertising. After all, advertisers must attract the ATTENTION of the public, and natural innovation and creativity would be essential. With the help of his father, who was desperate for him to find work, he landed a job in a large advertising firm.

Burton did very well in advertising. He worked for a woman who knew the ropes and was able to harness his creative energies. True to form, Burton became the "office clown" and managed to stimulate gales of laughter while attracting considerable ATTENTION.

Without much warning, the advertising firm lost a very large contract. This event was followed by a major reorganization causing many in key positions to lose their jobs. With the reshuffling of employees, Burton emerged as a vice president and head of a major division of the firm. At long last, Burton had become a leader! Leaders get ATTENTION! Burton was convinced that his behavior had been the key to his success; he decided to continue his ATTENTION-WINNING ways. He went out and purchased a wardrobe that many would consider "extreme".

Burton's initial meeting with his new subordinates was categorized by some as "very underwhelming". His attire seemed inappropriate for a person in his position of responsibility BUT IT DID GET THEIR ATTENTION. Burton began his address with an optimistic and upbeat theme that seemed to be encouraging. However, as he got "up to speed", the real Burton emerged–his "ribald revelry" came to the fore. With one joke he alienated all of the women in the room; he took care of the minorities with the next; the last one left the employee in a wheelchair in a rage. Burton attributed the gasps, rather than the expected laughs, to the fact that the group was new and just needed to get acquainted. For sure, he'd warm them up after a while. He tried for an hour, but they departed the meeting cold–very cold.

Sensing that his staff was too "up tight" to be effective, Burton launched into a concentrated "creative clowning" routine that he considered hilariously funny. At every opportunity, he told jokes, mimicked people and engaged in silly behavior. After all, such behavior won him ATTENTION and general approval when he was just another employee. For some reason not fully understood by Burton, their reactions were different–they didn't fully appreciate what he was doing.

The recovery of the firm after the loss of the major contract depended considerably on the reestablishment of a favorable image with potential customers. Burton, recognizing this and needing more ATTENTION, volunteered to organize and conduct a major promotion campaign. What followed proved to be the demise of the organization. Burton's antics–exaggerated, tasteless and considered childless by most–turned potential customers to stone. His subordinates watched silently and helplessly in total humiliation. Burton got the ATTENTION he was seeking; the firm got ATTENTION in the local press when it finally filed for bankruptcy.

LEADERS PROJECT AN ORGANIZATIONAL IMAGE

"HE'S A GOOD DON, BUT I'D FEEL BETTER IF HE PLAYED THE PART."

WHAT'S GOING ON HERE? WHY IS THIS HAPPENING?

Leaders serve many roles. One of these is the figurehead of the organization. Burton was entertaining and popular while he was serving in a subordinate or a peer capacity. However, when he became a leader, the expectations of others in the organization changed. Leaders must be role models whom subordinates expect and respect. Whereas some charismatic leaders are granted some "idiosyncracy credit" (the right to be "different")[2] by subordinates, they go too far if they project images that reflect unfavorably on the organization and its people.

WHAT SHOULD YOU DO IF YOU RECOGNIZE SOME OF THE CHARACTERISTICS OF BURTON BUFFOON IN YOURSELF?

Beware of being too much of an individualist. Recognize that when you engage in "extreme" behavior, you risk not only personal embarrassment but also the humiliation of those who serve you and depend on your good judgment. While leaders have some freedom that others don't, remember that there are some requirements for conformity. "Test the water" carefully to determine the appropriate range of acceptable behavior.

WHAT SHOULD YOU DO IF YOU DISCOVER SOME OF THE CHARACTERISTICS OF BURTON BUFFOON IN YOUR SUBORDINATES?

While you should allow subordinates the freedom to "be themselves", you should, tactfully and confidentially, intervene when subordinates exceed the "envelope" of acceptable behavior.

Sometimes it's a good idea to have some "organizational clowns" around to help with morale so long as they aren't offensive.

WHAT SHOULD YOU DO IF YOU'RE WORKING FOR A BOSS WITH SOME OF THE CHARACTERISTICS OF BURTON BUFFOON?

If Burton is otherwise a good person and the problem is bad judgment, I think you owe it to him to let him know when he's gone too far. This could be very risky, but the entire organization could be affected adversely by Burton's mistakes. If Burton is otherwise talented but mildly eccentric and slightly "way out", perhaps your best bet is to smile at his jokes and give him the ATTENTION he is seeking. Maybe your definition of "acceptable behavior" is too constrained.

NOTES

[1]Wess Roberts, *Leadership Secrets of Attila the Hun* (New York: Warner Books, 1985), p. 53.

[2]Office of Military Leadership, U.S. Military Academy, *A Study of Organizational Leadership* (Harrisburg, PA: Stackpole Books, 1976), p. 240.

If you receive this through the mail, it is possible that someone is telling you something about your style of leadership as perceived by others. Perhaps you should read *Paul Malone's* first book on leadership, **Love 'Em and Lead 'Em** (Synergy Press, 3420 Holly Road, Annandale, VA 22003 — $10.95 plus $1.50 postage).

(FOLD HERE)

FROM: (Optional)

____

____

____

PLACE STAMP HERE

TO: ______________________________

____

____

____

(Staple Here)

CHAPTER FOURTEEN

LEADERS DON'T EAT QUICHE

"Leadership should not be confused with the making of loud noises, profane comments or obscene gestures." (BIG BOOK, Small Paul to the Hell's Angels, 16:47)

"Women who compete like men are considered unfeminine. Women who emphasize family are considered uncommitted."

Felice N. Schwartz[1]

From the very day she was born, Tess Terone was described as "super feminine". Anyone visiting the nursery of Mercy Hospital readily recognized her as a "beautiful little baby girl".

Tess's orientation toward "feminine pursuits" seemed to stay with her. As a little girl, she was particularly attracted to dolls with frilly clothing, doll houses and the virtually unlimited variety of "homemaker" toys sold in the stores at outrageous prices. From the beginning, Tess was clothes-conscious. At three, she refused to wear long pants, insisting instead on pretty dresses accompanied by shiny shoes and frilly socks. In nursery school, she selected her

MOTHER

playmates carefully–other little girls who shared her fascination for things feminine. Tess became aware of another group at school that seemed to behave very differently according to a totally alien value system–little boys. These creatures seemed to make great quantities of noise. Further, they were attracted to mess, dirt and undisciplined behavior–very unfeminine. **Tess noted this and kept it in her heart.**

Tess retained her feminine orientation throughout her experience in the public school system. She was attracted to opportunities to learn ballet and how to play the violin. She applied herself with great vigor to these skills and developed considerable expertise. She selected her friends carefully–other girls with similar interests and pursuits.

Tess was an intense observer. From the time she learned to write, she recorded her observations in a diary. Further, she was continually developing personal conclusions regarding life in general based on these observations.

Tess continued to watch another group at school that stimulated her interest–boys. Most of them seemed to behave according to some outlandish rules of behavior. First off, they were just plain gross. They were loud, boisterous and insensitive. At first, their conversation consisted of "bathroom talk"; as they grew older, they added a litany of profanity and obscenities. They continued to be attracted to dirt and mud. Many signed up to play on the football team where they sweated profusely, made "oof"ing sounds as they collided with one another and emerged from the playing field uttering obscenities and all covered with mud. The strange thing that Tess couldn't comprehend was the fact that their behavior seemed to contribute to general approval. Further, these same "slime wallowers" with their foul mouths appeared to be selected for honors and highly prestigious positions. **Tess wrote these observations in her diary and kept them in her heart.**

Tess went on to college. She continued her interests in ballet and the violin and added drama. Her friends were confined to a small group that shared these pursuits. A few males were included.

However, Tess noted that these males received comparatively little public attention when compared to an animal-like group known as the "jocks". Most of these "jocks" were now huge men who went to great efforts to expand their muscles and distort their bodies. Their necks literally extended beyond their earlobes. They sweated more than ever, continued to get filthy on the playing field and often drank beer to excess at parties. Strangely enough, they seemed to command respect and attention—even many of the women were attracted to them. **Tess wrote these observations in her diary and kept them in her heart.**

After college, Tess went on to get a job. She was an extraordinarily hard worker. When given a task, she accomplished it with flawless perfection. Within months, the unique quality of her work was recognized throughout the firm. On one occasion, Tess "lost her cool" when those around her didn't contribute their fair share to a project. In the process, she even uttered a mild obscenity. This seemed to get people's attention. **Tess recorded this in her diary and kept it in her heart.**

Tess noted that, whereas the work force of the firm was equally divided between men and women, the leadership positions were all filled by men. Further, these men seemed to have some characteristics in common. They were aggressive, assertive and very demanding. When upset, they could become very intimidating. **Tess wrote these observations in her diary and kept them in her heart.**

It was time for the firm's annual Christmas party. Tess dreaded the thought of it. Last year, many of the male bosses drank too much and made fools of themselves. However, Tess knew it was a "command performance"; her boss would be furious if everyone didn't attend.

After an hour of intense drinking and the consumption of stale hors d'oeuvres, the president of the firm began to make his traditional Christmas address. However, from the beginning, it was clear that he had something unusual on his mind. Instead of exhorting people on to loftier goals, he spoke of reorganization. He mentioned the imminent retirement of several top executives and readjustments in the organizational hierarchy. Then, came the bombshell! He recognized that the firm had been negligent in providing promotional opportunities for women. He followed with an announcement of a series of promotions <u>that included Tess</u>! Tess had been promoted to the position of chief of a branch with 40 people! As the applause subsided, Tess wandered out of the party room in total disbelief.

Tess returned to her apartment and immediately consulted her diary. After several hours of thoughtful analysis, she reached the following conclusions:

- **It's still a man's world.**
- **Men are aggressive, demanding, coarse and gross.**
- **Occasionally, women get a chance to lead.**
- **Women in leadership positions must emulate men in order to be effective.**

The next Monday morning, Tess requested a vacation. Since she had used none of her vacation up to that point, she was able to take a month off. She decided to use that month to prepare for her responsibilities as a leader of subordinates. She referred frequently to her diary as she developed her master plan.

Tess decided right off that, unless she could locate a completely domesticated male, marriage and children would not be for her. Then she examined herself in the mirror. Whereas her slim body elicited occasional male whistles at the beach, it was totally inappropriate for a leader. What she needed was bulk; people respect bigness. Since growing taller was out of the question, she concluded that some appropriate filling out was in order. After considerable searching, she discovered the solution to her dilemma–Mother Macho's Assertiveness Agency.

Tess arrived at Mother Macho's totally committed to preparing for her new role. After an initial indoctrination, Tess was exposed to countless hours of viewing professional football, hockey and wrestling contests while consuming great quantities of potato chips and beer. She learned to belch and make strange bodily noises. During intervening periods she took steroids and worked out lifting barbells, developing her arms and shoulders. In particular, she was seeking to develop large veins in her arms that could be admired by others. She participated in courses focusing on various forms of obscenities and learned the "big seven" words for general use plus twenty terms for special occasions. She took a seminar on dirty jokes conducted by a particularly crude humorist whose presentations were at scream level. She participated in a speech therapy course focusing on deepening her voice and creating intimidating situations. As she gained weight and added bulk to her body, it became necessary to replace her wardrobe. She purchased several suits with severe lines and massive shoulder pads at Wallach's and Barney's in New York. Tess stopped shaving her armpits and legs and tried unsuccessfully to stimulate body hair using concoctions designed to stop male baldness. She considered a tattoo, but concluded that this might be going too far; it could cause problems in a nursing home later in life. Within a month, Tess was an entirely different woman, one totally prepared for her new leadership responsibilities.

Tess's return to the firm and to her new job after the month at Mother Macho's was nothing short of momentous. Her fellow workers hardly recognized her. Her first staff conference, where she stiff-armed one of the older men who attempted to hold the door for her and then demonstrated her new voice and vocabulary, drew gasps that could be heard throughout the building.

Needless to say, the "new Tess" had a profound effect on the organization and its employees. There was no question concerning who was in charge. Goals and objectives were clearly and profanely defined; standards were established; very little was left to the imagination. After the initial "shock period", a few employees departed; others adapted and continued to earn their daily bread.

WHAT'S GOING ON HERE? WHY IS THIS HAPPENING?

Obviously, Tess's example is a gross exaggeration designed to amuse (some won't be amused at all). It is totally unlikely that anyone would "change her stripes" to this degree during mid-life regardless of circumstances. However, there is some difference of opinion concerning the proper roles of women in leadership positions. In a working world still dominated by men, how should women who get the chance to lead behave? Can they be themselves or must they adopt the "characteristics of men" in order to be effective? Must women give up families and children in order to be competitive? I don't presume to have the answer. Until we overcome some problems with "sexual stereotypes" in the minds of many—both men and women—the problem will remain unresolved. Women wrestling with this problem should consider reading Marilyn Loden's book, *Feminine Leadership or How to Succeed in Business Without Being One of the Boys.*[2]

WHAT SHOULD YOU DO IF YOU RECOGNIZE SOME OF THE CHARACTERISTICS OF TESS TERONE IN YOURSELF?

I'll address this response to women. I believe that the style of leadership that works best for you is a function of your unique personality.[3] With this in mind, don't try to be someone else as Tess has done. While most leaders must be assertive, demanding and decisive at times, women who are feminine can develop these characteristics as well as anyone else.

WHICH WAY WOMEN???

WHAT SHOULD YOU DO IF YOU DISCOVER SOME OF THE CHARACTERISTICS OF TESS TERONE IN YOUR SUBORDINATES?

I'll address this response to both men and women. I'd say do nothing unless the behavior is bothering others in the organization. In many cases, people with "extreme" behavior change when they sense the disapproval of their peers. If you have to take action, do it sensitively and privately.

WHAT SHOULD YOU DO IF YOU'RE WORKING FOR A BOSS WITH SOME OF THE CHARACTERISTICS OF TESS TERONE?

I guess it all depends on your individual value system. Personally, I'd be uncomfortable since Tess's behavior doesn't fit my image of a woman in any role including that of a leader. However, those involved in professional mud wrestling and roller derbies might find Tess's style very appropriate. I'd just continue to be myself and adapt to working for Tess. However, I don't think I'd invite her to the ballet or the opera.

NOTES

[1]Felice N. Schwartz, "Management Women and the New Facts of Life", *Harvard Business Review*, January/February, 1989, pp. 65-76.

[2]Marilyn Loden, *Feminine Leadership or How to Succeed in Business Without Being One of the Boys* (New York: Times Books, 1985).

[3]Paul B. Malone III, *Love 'Em and Lead 'Em* (Annandale, VA: Synergy Press, 1986).

If you receive this through the mail, it is possible that someone is telling you something about your style of leadership as perceived by others. Perhaps you should read *Paul Malone's* first book on leadership, **Love 'Em and Lead 'Em** (Synergy Press, 3420 Holly Road, Annandale, VA 22003 — $10.95 plus $1.50 postage).

(FOLD HERE)

FROM: (Optional)

____

____

____

PLACE STAMP HERE

TO: ____________________________________

____

____

____

(Staple Here)

CHAPTER FIFTEEN

A CRISIS A DAY KEEPS PROFITS AWAY

"Overreacting contributes to a sour stomach and a zig-zag path into the future." (BIG BOOK, Small Paul to the Knee-Jerk Neurotics, 18:63)

"Everything good in life stands on the razor-edge of danger."

Thornton Wilder in *Skin of Our Teeth*[1]

"An attitude some call FUD—fear, uncertainty and doubt—is the nemesis of the tough-minded optimism that sustains renewal."

Warren Bennis and Burt Nanus[2]

Kassandra Kaos looked up from the newspaper. She exclaimed, "My God! This government report concludes that much of the poultry in the United States isn't inspected and that unsanitary chickens could result in major problems with food poisoning! Chicken won't sell; we're in the wrong business!" Kassandra then directed her secretary to contact all managers and staff of Chickoyummy Kitchens to attend an emergency meeting at 6:00 p.m. that day.

Kassandra's secretary responded stoically and referred to a list

CRISIS
CRISIS
CRISIS
CRISIS
CRISIS
CRISIS
PHalons

of telephone numbers. "Emergency meetings" had become routine in the firm since Kassandra had become President. Chickoyummy Kitchens was a brand new name for a reasonably successful corporation that originally served a variety of fast foods at twenty-five establishments in the Southeastern United States. When Kassandra took charge, she had become infatuated by the clever commercials of Frank Perdue and the unusual things he did to chickens. Kassandra became convinced that chicken was the wave of the future in the fast food business. At a previous emergency meeting, Kassandra transmitted this guidance. With this, a new name, Chickoyummy Kitchens, emerged, and the organization adapted to focus on one primary product.

Kassandra began the meeting precisely at 6:00 p.m., addressing a group of twenty people who were very obviously exhausted: "Ladies and gentlemen, we have a major crisis on our hands. I've just read a report that gives chicken a bad name. We must respond quickly and get out of the chicken business or we're all doomed!"

Caught by surprise, the group gasped almost in unison. They had been too busy recently to read the paper. They had been involved in the massive reorganization associated with changing the name to Chickoyummy Kitchens and modifying facilities to focus on a single product. Finally, one manager responded, "Kassandra, do you realize what this means? Our logo is a chicken; there's a brand new, 25-foot sign in the shape of a smiling chicken on every shop. We have chicken menus, chicken costumes and our equipment is designed to prepare chicken. Those reports come out all of the time. Before long, every food will be condemned by someone or another."

Kassandra, brandishing the newspaper article, was resolute. She had a lot of financial leverage in the company. The meeting went on until well after midnight with everyone recognizing that, indeed, there was a crisis at hand. Eventually, substitutes to chicken were explored. Duck was suggested since possibly the 25-foot signs could be modified to look like ducks. However, the logo, Duckoyummy, had little appeal and ducks were notoriously greasy.

Finally, in the wee hours of the morning, it was agreed that losses would be minimized if the firm returned to its original business of selling a variety of fast foods. Totally exhausted, the group returned to their homes for some sleep while developing lists of things that had to be done and undone.

While Kassandra's subordinates put in many long hours responding to this new guidance, events leading to what was known as the "poisons crises" unfolded. It seemed that Kassandra was attracted to a publicity campaign, the one with Ed McMahon's picture. In the process, she subscribed to many new magazines, among them those focusing on health. Articles in these magazines attracted Kassandra's attention and immediate alarm. One focused on the dangers of caffeine. This promoted an emergency meeting that resulted in the elimination of all beverages containing caffeine from the menu. In short succession, there were emergency meetings eliminating saccharin, eggs, milk products and all foods containing animal fats. By this time, Kassandra's numb subordinates dutifully responded by eliminating the offensive material of the day and adapting to what foods were left. Fancy menus were replaced by photocopy versions as the environment became more and more dynamic. The problem was that Kassandra's establishments offered very little variety, and sales were declining dramatically.

Kassandra presided over an emergency meeting at 8:00 p.m. The emergency of the day was the monthly report of revenues and costs. Kassandra was alarmed; the firm was clearly going down the tubes. She referred to a recent issue of a health magazine and declared, "You know, it's clear that we are in the wrong business. America is health-conscious. People get healthy through exercise, not by gorging themselves. Health spas are in. Now we have twenty-five locations that could be readily converted into athletic facilities." While Kassandra's voice droned on into the night, members of her staff exited individually or in small groups, some to read up on health spas, most to seek other employment.

WHAT'S GOING ON HERE? WHY IS THIS HAPPENING?

Kassandra's style could be classified as "leadership by crisis". The trouble is that, in Kassandra's view, **virtually everything is a crisis.** She is overreacting to events in a world influenced by an "information explosion". Leaders do need a sense of urgency and an ability to redirect their organizations in response to a changing world. However, there's a limit to how much change an organization and its people can endure. Clearly, Kassandra has exceeded this limit. Decisions often involve major investments and sunk costs that cannot be retrieved; these must be acknowledged before they are sacrificed and new directions are selected. Kassandra's subordinates are totally confused. Those who stay with Kassandra are likely to become "numb" and uncommitted to any plan since it's likely that another "crisis" will result in a brand new plan.

WHAT SHOULD YOU DO IF YOU RECOGNIZE SOME OF THE CHARACTERISTICS OF KASSANDRA KAOS IN YOURSELF?

First, recognize that leaders of today, in a world dominated by change, must serve as organizational "engines of change". However, they must realize that much of the information reaching them is likely to be misleading, totally false or subject to change itself. With this in mind, leaders must develop "conceptual skills"—the ability to interpret information, analyze its significance, and visualize its effect on the future.

Next, leaders must appreciate the fact that plans are **decisions now concerning the future** (the future is <u>not</u> completely predictable) and that they involve investments. Plans also involve the commitment and energies of people. Of course, **no plan goes precisely according to plan**, but it does provide basic direction.

Finally, leaders must recognize that most change is threatening to people; it forces them out of the *status quo* into the terrors of the unknown. In his book, *Future Shock*, Alvin Toffler described the destabilizing effect of rapid change on people.[3] Niccolò Machiavelli noted this in 1513 when he observed:

> **There is nothing more difficult to carry out, nor more doubtful of success, nor more dangerous to handle, than to initiate a new order of things. For the reformer has enemies in all who profit by the old order and only luke-warm defenders in all those who would profit by the new order. This luke-warmness arises partly from fear of their adversaries who have the law in their favor; and partly from the incredulity of mankind, who do not truly believe in anything new until they have had actual experience of it.**[4]

If you resemble Kassandra Kaos, try to reduce your anxieties, recognize that many "crises" are grossly overstated, work hard to develop good plans, and, finally, give those good plans chances to germinate. You can always "tweak" your plans (make minor adjustments) rather than heading off in an entirely new direction. By all means, give your subordinates chances to participate in the planning process.

WHAT SHOULD YOU DO IF YOU DISCOVER SOME OF THE CHARACTERISTICS OF KASSANDRA KAOS IN YOUR SUBORDINATES?

Much of what was said in the preceding paragraphs applies in this case. Remember that you, as the leader, should transmit a spirit of optimism unless the sky is beginning to fall. Do your best to reduce their anxieties and to create a feeling of confidence within the organization. Remember that the **will to succeed** is an essential ingredient to success.

WHAT SHOULD YOU DO IF YOU'RE WORKING FOR A BOSS WITH SOME OF THE CHARACTERISTICS OF KASSANDRA KAOS?

Be prepared for some chaotic and frustrating times. Maintain your "cool", do your "homework" and provide good advice concerning the "right" course of action. In some cases, you can help a lot by reducing your boss's anxieties and trying to give him or her some confidence. If you have subordinates, do your best to tend to their anxieties and, if possible, to explain WHY things are happening as they are.

NOTES

[1]Henry M. Wriston, "Rugged Individualism", Annie Talbot Cole Lecture, 1970, p. 15.

[2]Warren Bennis and Burt Nanus, *Leaders* (New York: Harper & Row, 1985).

[3]Alvin Toffler, *Future Shock* (New York: Random House, Inc., 1970).

[4]Niccolò Machiavelli, *The Prince and the Discourses*, Introduction by Max Lerner (New York: The Modern Library, 1940), p. 21.

If you receive this through the mail, it is possible that someone is telling you something about your style of leadership as perceived by others. Perhaps you should read *Paul Malone's* first book on leadership, **Love 'Em and Lead 'Em** (Synergy Press, 3420 Holly Road, Annandale, VA 22003 — $10.95 plus $1.50 postage).

(FOLD HERE)

FROM: (Optional)

____

____

____

PLACE
STAMP
HERE

TO: ____________________________________

____

____

____

(Staple Here)

CHAPTER SIXTEEN

THE STAIN OF GLOOM

"For many people life literally sucks! Leaders can change that." (BIG BOOK, Small Paul to the Morbid Morticians, 45:99)

"Excellence is optimistic. It's believing that something can be done, that it's worth fighting for, worth trusting others to play a part."

Tom Peters and Nancy Austin[1]

The flight attendants of the Boeing 747 assembled excitedly in the crew's lounge at Kennedy International Airport. This flight was to be an unusual treat–a flight to Honolulu, Hawaii, with a three-day layover! This was a special charter flight; the crew had not worked together before. Gladys, the head cabin attendant, exclaimed, "Three days in the sun in the middle of a soggy winter; what a deal!" She held up the tiny bathing suit she planned to wear; everyone laughed merrily.

The flight engineer of Trans-Galactic Flight 1099 joined the group. He had just completed the preflight inspection of the aircraft. He commented, "That airplane is really in tip-top shape! It just came out of a major overhaul." He went on to introduce himself to the others in the crew.

The next to arrive was the first officer and copilot, carrying a leather bag filled with maps, charts and flight navigation manuals. "It's going to be a real dream flight, folks. Just about perfect

GLOOM

weather all along our route!" He joined the group that engaged in animated conversation concerning what to do in Honolulu at this time of year.

The first officer looked up and spotted a man standing at the edge of the crowd. He said, "Ladies and gentlemen, this is our captain for the flight, Captain Blair Despair! Good morning, Captain Despair. I'm Robert Rudder, your copilot. These folks are your crew for Flight 1099. It's indeed a pleasure to meet you! We're all certainly looking forward to this flight!"

"Flying is deadly serious business!" replied Captain Despair with a growl and a look of melancholy that turned the crew to stone. "Explosions, charred remains, body bags, endless investigations", he continued. "Don't any of you forget that we're pushing the odds every minute we fly. Young woman, put that obscene bathing suit away."

Gladys blushed profusely and complied.

"Mr. Rudder, what aircraft have we been assigned for the flight?" asked the captain.

Robert Rudder replied, "It's tail number 29477, sir; she's just come out of . . ."

"That piece of junk!" interrupted Despair in total disgust. "That airplane is 17 years old. It's nothing but a flying time bomb!"

"But sir, it's just come out of a major overhaul; some of the systems are brand new; the navigation system is the very best the airline has", Rudder responded defensively.

"All done by a bunch of incompetents and misfits, half of whom are probably on drugs! They drop their tools and their sack lunches in the engine openings and leave half of the hatches unsecured", roared Despair at the top of his voice. He went to a white telephone and engaged in a prolonged conversation with the Director of Operations, demanding another aircraft—all while the crew listened in silence. After what seemed an eternity, he hung up in disgust, apparently convinced that a substitute aircraft was unavailable. "Rudder, I want you to conduct another preflight inspection—A THOROUGH ONE. I'll be with you shortly. As for the rest of you in the crew, I have one bit of advice—CAUTION. Check everything; don't leave anything to chance." He turned to Rudder again, "What's the en route weather like?"

"Almost perfect, Captain, even around San Francisco where we'll be refueling", Rudder replied, seeking some break in the gloom.

Despair rolled his eyes and grimaced, "Perfect weather! The worst kind! That's when some front whips in and catches you by surprise. It'll be just our luck to have an earthquake while we're on the ground in San Francisco!"

Despair left the group without further comment to inspect the aircraft. Most of the others moved silently to rest rooms in the vicinity; some became sick. Those in the ladies' room could hear through an open window a violent argument between Despair and the maintenance personnel on the tarmac below.

Preparations for the departure of Trans-Galactic Flight 1099 continued without major incident. Captain Despair, citing warnings of a bomb scare that did not exist, spent considerable time in the passenger waiting room examining the excited Hawaii-bound vacationers who belonged to the Horney Holidays Travel Club, a group of military retirees and their spouses whose motto was "pack your socks and get off your rocks". He insisted that a tiny lady in her eighties be searched by security guards because she had a tape recorder in her travel bag. His dour observation was overheard by several passengers: "This flight is packed with people and fuel; she'll go down like a stone if there's engine trouble." This led to a few seeking alternate transportation.

Preparations completed, passengers boarded Flight 1099. They were greeted by courteous but obviously apprehensive flight attendants whose anxious looks transmitted messages that dampened the spirits of even the heartiest vacationer. What followed was an uneasy flight that seemed to last forever, with many of the passengers recounting their sins and praying a lot. Those who drank, drank more than normal and tried to sleep. Those who remained awake will never forget the ghostly view of the Captain wandering the aisles, obviously searching for catastrophes waiting to happen. Further, his comment over the public address system in a voice that seemed to be coming from the bottom of a well, "This is your captain. We are en route at 35,000 feet. We have no concrete evidence of aircraft problems or a bomb threat. Have a nice flight and keep your seat belts on at all times", did nothing to stimulate confidence.

Flight 1099 arrived in Honolulu on time. Passengers silently exited the aircraft, totally ignoring the Hawaiian dancers assigned to greet them on arrival. Some were seen making signs of the cross and kissing the ground. The crew followed them, grim, tense and unsmiling. While they had three days in Honolulu ahead of them, they were contemplating the return trip under the command of Captain Blair Despair.

WHAT'S GOING ON HERE? WHY IS THIS HAPPENING?

Obviously, Blair Despair is a gloomy and pessimistic person. Let me admit that this case is very unrealistic; not many real pessimists who value their lives take up flying for a living.

Leaders must recognize that, since they possess power, they influence the working lives of subordinates directly and, indirectly, even their private lives. Whether leaders realize it or not, subordinates observe them and interpret the "messages" (verbal and non-verbal) they transmit. In this particular case, Blair's "stain of gloom" was transmitted to the entire crew. This "stain" affected their attitudes and their behavior.

WHAT SHOULD YOU DO IF YOU RECOGNIZE SOME OF THE CHARACTERISTICS OF BLAIR DESPAIR IN YOURSELF?

If this is the real you, I guess there's nothing much you can do about it. However, if there's a choice, I recommend that you change your behavior, at least in the presence of subordinates. For many people, life is not a particularly pleasant experience. You, the leader, influence a significant major part of your subordinates' lives. I think you owe it to them to make that part as pleasant as possible. If you can, become a "ray of sunshine" even when things are tough. Not only will you do your subordinates some good, but your subordinates are likely to express their appreciation in the form of favorable attitudes and desirable work performance.

WHAT SHOULD YOU DO IF YOU DISCOVER SOME OF THE CHARACTERISTICS OF BLAIR DESPAIR IN YOUR SUBORDINATES?

Since gloom is infectious, I would go to some efforts to find out what is wrong and try to help correct the situation. Maybe some sort of frivolous event would help "loosen" people up. However, recognize that, for some, gloom is a way of life. There are many people totally committed to the philosophy that "life sucks!" Try to place the gloomy people in the organization where they'll do the least damage.

WHAT SHOULD YOU DO IF YOU'RE WORKING FOR A BOSS WITH SOME OF THE CHARACTERISTICS OF BLAIR DESPAIR?

Recognize that, no matter how hard you resist, some of that gloom is likely to affect you. If you can, see if you can identify the causes and perhaps reduce the pessimistic tendencies. Do your best to maintain the morale of those around you. If you sense that this is impossible and that your life is being adversely affected, leave the organization and find some "sunshine" elsewhere.

NOTES

[1]Tom Peters and Nancy Austin, *A Passion for Excellence* (New York: Random House, 1985), p. 417.

THE LEADER

A RAY OF SUNSHINE IN A GLOOMY WORLD

If you receive this through the mail, it is possible that someone is telling you something about your style of leadership as perceived by others. Perhaps you should read *Paul Malone's* first book on leadership, **Love 'Em and Lead 'Em** (Synergy Press, 3420 Holly Road, Annandale, VA 22003 — $10.95 plus $1.50 postage).

(FOLD HERE)

FROM: (Optional)

____

____

____

PLACE
STAMP
HERE

TO: ____________________________________

____

____

____

(Staple Here)

CHAPTER SEVENTEEN

SCREAMING WITHOUT MEANING

"A decision not to make a decision is a decision." (BIG BOOK, Small Paul to the Society of Procrastinators, 78:36).

"To talk much and arrive nowhere is the same as climbing a tree to catch a fish."
Chinese Proverb[1]

"Communication! Daddy, organizational communication is the lifeblood of any organization! Ninety percent of problems in organizations are the direct result of inadequate communication!" declared Pam Demonium with great enthusiasm.

Sam Demonium, Pam's father, nodded and continued to try to study monthly sales reports in preparation for tomorrow's meeting. Pam's diatribe had been going on for two hours now. It seemed that, since she had begun her Master of Business Administration program at a prestigious northeastern university, she had become an eminent authority on the subject of business management. Sam was exhausted from a busy week and dreaded the thought of tomorrow's Saturday morning staff meeting that was sure to go on into the evening. He anticipated major disagreements concerning problems his firm faced.

Pam continued, "I've discussed your management techniques with Professor Sensitivo, my instructor in organizational dynamics.

He says you're a product of the Stone Age and even hinted that you should go to jail for some of the things you do."

A bit irritated by Pam's comment, Sam looked up and asked, "What has this guy, Sensitivo, ever done?"

"He wrote the textbook we use in class!" replied Pam proudly.

"Oh, yeah, the one that set me back $39.95!" recalled Sam with a bit of remorse. As he remembered, the book entitled *Management Is Easy* contained only 200 pages.

Sam attempted to redirect his attention to the sales report in his hand. Sam Demonium was President and Chief Operating Officer of Barfunckle's, a chain of department stores in the middle-eastern United States. This firm had managed to retain its family-owned status and remain profitable throughout turbulent economic times and several attempts at mergers and acquisitions by large conglomerates. Sam, a divorcé, was in his late fifties. Pam, his only child, 24 years old, was living with him while she participated in an MBA program at a local university at prices that made even a wealthy man like Sam wince. Pam had become intensely interested in Barfunckle's. On several occasions, Sam had offered his daughter opportunities to work in one of the stores in entry-level positions. However, she repeatedly declined, declaring that "working in the trenches" would contaminate her conceptual approach to business. Pam's future was uncertain. Recently, she had mentioned interest in a law degree after her MBA, and then there was always her fascination for medicine.

Seeking some privacy to continue his reading, Sam went to the bathroom. Obviously, Pam was not prepared to discontinue her discussion. She spoke through the door loudly, "Daddy, you've got to open up your organizational communications. You've got to start listening to people. Just think, Daddy, if you'd listened better, you'd still be married to Mommy!"

Pam's final comment got his attention. His former wife, Dora, had run off with a salesman from a competing firm, citing his preoccupation with business and his severe dandruff condition as factors contributing to her dissatisfaction. He called pleasantly through the door, "Pam, I'll see what I can do to improve. Meanwhile I've got to get ready for tomorrow's meeting."

Sam Demonium continued as president of Barfunckle's for another year while his daughter completed her MBA. Meanwhile, at an annual clothing manufacturers' convention, Sam met an extremely attractive young woman, Theresa Torso. Theresa was an aspiring actress who had played a supporting role in a creative movie titled *Debbie Does the United States Senate*. Sam fell desperately in love with Theresa. He decided that 35 years of hard labor was enough and that he would retire, marry this sweet young thing and spend the remainder of his life in ethereal bliss.

When Sam approached the Board of Directors with his retirement decision, the subject of his successor came up. Sam observed that the firm was dominated by old-fashioned thinking and that it needed young blood and modern management ideas. After some discussion, Pam's name was suggested. Finally, due in large part to the respect of the members of the board for Sam, it was decided that Pam Demonium would be the next President of Barfunckle's.

Pam received the news with great enthusiasm and tore up her applications to law schools. She consulted with Professor Sensitivo and several other faculty members at the business school. She prepared her comments for her first meeting with the staff at Barfunckle's.

"Communication! Organizational communication is the lifeblood of any organization! Ninety percent of problems in any organization are the result of inadequate communication!" declared Pam confidently to the assembled staff of Barfunckle's at her introductory meeting. She pursued this theme for over an hour citing contemporary management theorists, William Ouchi's *Theory Z*[2], *The One Minute Manager*[3] and a number of recent books on human behavior. In the process, Pam declared that her door was always open and that she planned to practice "Management by Walking Around"[4]. Further, she identified Barfunckle's problem—"information thrombosis"—a problem that she planned to resolve through a program called "information saturation". The initial meeting terminated abruptly when the public address system broke down and employees began to leave. Strangely, Pam continued to speak for several minutes before she was aware that the crowd was thinning out.

Reaction to Pam's speech varied from total disinterest to some enthusiasm. Saul Soul, a vice president who had hoped to succeed to Sam Demonium's position, attempted to define "information saturation". Seeking to win Pam's immediate favor, he directed that the weekly business summary, which up to then had been distributed only to division and branch managers, now be provided to all 9,000 of Barfunckle's employees. Since this computer printout consisted of 30 pages, photocopying costs skyrocketed.

For the next week, Pam spent 18-hour days visiting Barfunckle's ten stores, chatting exhaustively with employees on a variety of subjects, including their personal lives, and combatting the evils of "information thrombosis". She then indicated that she was not seeing enough of her immediate staff. Saul Soul responded with a decision to change staff meetings from weekly to daily. This appeared to satisfy Pam; daily staff meetings involved discussions that went on for hours. Pam suggested that her staff use the same approach within their branches and divisions. Further, Pam noted that partitions within office spaces constituted "psychological barriers" to honest, candid communications. Within a day, Saul Soul had them removed. Noise levels increased considerably in work spaces; this pleased Pam; "information saturation" was working!

These were turbulent times in the retail trade industry. Competitors were making inroads, vendors were going in and out of business, styles were changing. It was time for critical top-level decisions. A series of decision briefings were planned. Typically, at these briefings, the responsible staff member would make a presentation providing the facts, analyzing the alternatives available to the firm and making a recommendation.

Pam's reactions to these meetings were consistent: "Well, I don't know. Have you considered everything? We don't seem to have enough information. Let's study it further."

Saul Soul, responding to Pam's "Let's study it further" guidance, initiated a comprehensive program of in-depth organizational analysis. What resulted was a series of "skunk works", "think tanks" and special committees designed to analyze virtually every subject requiring either attention or inattention. Pam approved of this initiative and reminded Saul that <u>everyone</u> in the organization should be consulted. Barfunckle's organizational structure changed dramatically as virtually every employee belonged to one or more *ad hoc* organizations in addition to holding a regular job.

Employees were talking to one another as never before–**often at the expense of customers**. Desks and wastebaskets were piled with weekly reports that most employees did not have the time or the desire to read–they were doing so much talking. Meetings, often without agendas, went on for hours, often until fatigue overcame the participants. Many employees could not be located by their bosses since they spent so much time working in their *ad hoc* groups. Most importantly, **no major decisions were made**–all were deferred pending additional information and/or subsequent analysis. Lacking timely decisions, Barfunckle's maintained the *status quo* **WHILE THE WORLD ABOUT IT CHANGED.**

Pam's "information saturation" program lasted about six months. Business was bad; competition was keen. The Board of Directors, sensing that the retail business wasn't much fun anymore and that the timing was right, agreed to an offer to buy out the firm by a European conglomerate. Many of Barfunckle's managers lost their jobs; interestingly, Saul Soul survived and prospered. Pam, not particularly concerned, went off to law school totally convinced that "information thrombosis" is truly a dreaded organizational disease. Meanwhile, Sam Demonium and Theresa appear to be communicating effectively; they just announced the arrival of their third child.

WHAT'S GOING ON HERE? WHY IS THIS HAPPENING?

First off, let me acknowledge that this story is very unrealistic. It's unlikely that a firm of this size would be turned over to an inexperienced person–even one with an MBA from a prestigious university! (despite the expectations of some of the MBAs I've met).

Pam's story involves two interrelated factors associated with leadership–(1) the availability of information and (2) the use of information. Pam's goal–open two-way communication–is generally considered **GOOD**. Pam's hangup–a reluctance or an inability to make decisions–is generally considered **BAD**.

Most experts agree that timely and factual communication–upward, downward, sideward, diagonal–is vital; information is the "lifeblood" of an organization. People who know what's going on can operate like thinking, reasoning human beings–not like inanimate cogs in a machine. People who have a chance to contribute to decisions tend to be committed to those decisions. Most people like to be consulted; many problems can be identified and resolved by the people in "the trenches"–those actually doing the work. Bosses who "Manage by Walking Around" have access to information they would never receive cooped up in their offices.[5]

Talking and listening take time. Time is a precious commodity; it should be used productively. People in organizations must (1) gather information, (2) analyze information, (3) make decisions based on those analyses, (4) take action based on those decisions and (5) evaluate the impact of those decisions. Decisions involve risks since mortals cannot always predict the future accurately. Many bosses can't accept such risks and defer decisions pending the receipt of more complete information. These delays constitute decisions–"keep doing the same things". These "non-decisions" can be disastrous if the world changes and yesterday's correct decisions become today's mistakes.

WHAT SHOULD YOU DO IF YOU RECOGNIZE SOME OF THE CHARACTERISTICS OF PAM DEMONIUM IN YOURSELF?

By all means, encourage open and candid communication within your organization, but give that process purpose. Keep your door and your ears open and allocate time to visit with your employees and find out what's going on and why (some people call this "face time"). At the same time, develop the guts to make timely decisions based on the best available (albeit incomplete) information. Consider taking a course focusing on the decision-making process. If you can't bear to make decisions, delegate the authority to a trusted subordinate **but remember that, as the leader, you are responsible for everything the organization does or fails to do.** Try to delegate the near-time decisions to subordinates so that you can focus your thoughts farther into the future.

WHAT SHOULD YOU DO IF YOU DISCOVER SOME OF THE CHARACTERISTICS OF PAM DEMONIUM IN YOUR SUBORDINATES?

Again, encourage the communication process while insisting that the subordinates fulfill their decision making responsibilities. Provide encouragement and confidence; allow for some mistakes (non-catastrophic); if necessary, enroll them in courses that focus on the decision-making process. Recognize that, like tennis, decision making takes practice. If all of this fails, assign them to jobs that require no decisions.

WHAT SHOULD YOU DO IF YOU'RE WORKING FOR A BOSS WITH SOME OF THE CHARACTERISTICS OF PAM DEMONIUM?

First off, if you value your time, be prepared for humongous frustrations. Leaders with Pam's "decision-making" style can sometimes get away with it if the organizational environment is static and tranquil. However, Pam's approach can be the "kiss of death" in dynamic times. Perhaps you can assist by helping your boss develop confidence (develop scenarios, keep the number of alternatives manageable, establish decision deadlines). If this doesn't work, you might volunteer to make some of the decisions yourself (without embarrassing your boss). However, that can be very risky business if either your judgment or your luck is bad.

NOTES

[1]Joe D. Batten, *Tough-Minded Leadership* (New York: AMACOM, 1989), p. 64.

[2]William Ouchi, *Theory Z: How American Business Can Meet the Japanese Challenge* (Reading, MA: Addison-Wessley Publishing Company, 1981).

[3]Kenneth Blanchard and Spencer Johnson, *The One Minute Manager* (New York: William Morrow and Company, Inc., 1982).

[4]Tom Peters and Nancy Austin, *A Passion for Excellence* (New York: Random House, 1985), p. 6.

[5]For those who would like to read further into the complexities of understanding the great mass of information available and putting it to productive use, the author recommends Richard Saul Wurman's book, *Information Anxiety* (New York: Doubleday, 1989).

If you receive this through the mail, it is possible that someone is telling you something about your style of leadership as perceived by others. Perhaps you should read *Paul Malone's* first book on leadership, **Love 'Em and Lead 'Em** (Synergy Press, 3420 Holly Road, Annandale, VA 22003 — $10.95 plus $1.50 postage).

(FOLD HERE)

FROM: (Optional)

____

____

____

PLACE STAMP HERE

TO: ______________________________

____

____

____

(Staple Here)

CHAPTER EIGHTEEN

MOTHER 'EM AND SMOTHER 'EM

"He who treateth his subordinates as children should purchase many diapers." (BIG BOOK, Small Paul to the Fraternal Order of Meddling Managers, 29:83)

"The old models of leadership no longer work. In an age of individual rights, paternal protectors appear patronizing."
Michael Maccoby[1]

The two young women were chatting quietly as they smoked their cigarettes in the break area of Verna's Beauty Emporium. Business had been brisk, and they welcomed the chance to relax. Their conversation ceased as Verna Materna, the owner of the establishment, entered the room.

"Very bad habit, ladies!" noted Verna pleasantly. "Smoking stains your teeth, gives you bad breath, destroys your lungs, impairs your vision and makes you infertile." Verna, an ex-smoker herself, certainly knew what she was talking about. She continued for ten minutes about the evils of smoking. Both employees extinguished their cigarettes and listened attentively, agreeing that "Verna knows best". After that discussion, they limited their smoking to visits to their cars in the parking lot.

Verna's Beauty Emporium employed twenty cosmeticians and

hairdressers, mostly women, and was well-known in the area for the quality of its services. Verna paid her employees well; many had been working for her for years. In fact, many were considered to be "experts" in certain areas of beauty services.

Verna Materna was a very warm, congenial and caring person. She recognized her role as the leader of the organization and took her responsibilities very seriously. She took an intense personal interest in all of her employees. Since she was older than most, she sensed that she had an obligation to provide them inspiration and, more importantly, guidance. To Verna, the emporium was her "family". Since she had no children of her own, Verna's employees served as substitutes. Verna even took a long-term maternal interest in her frequent customers.

Verna was a very energetic and active person. Constantly on the go, she flitted from chair to chair, chatting with people, making corrections and ensuring that her warm, effervescent personality pervaded the premises.

She approached a female customer who was showing one of Verna's employees the hair style she preferred. "No, that just isn't you, Simone", observed Verna. Apparently, Simone disagreed; Simone knew what she wanted. A prolonged discussion followed with neither party yielding. The woman finally departed the shop to have her hair styled elsewhere. Verna bid her farewell warmly, satisfied that she had served a vital purpose. After all, "Verna knew best".

All new employees at the emporium received an orientation regarding hairdressing procedures. These were divided into three phases. Continuation from one phase to another required Verna's personal inspection and approval. These procedures applied to all employees regardless of experience level or duration of employment at Verna's. Some questioned the necessity of such scrutiny. Verna was firm; each step required her personal approval, inspiration and guidance. After all, in Verna's "family", "Mother knows best". A few of the highly skilled employees considered this "too much" and departed for other employment.

Separations such as these were always tearful occasions for Verna; she hated to see her "family" breaking up.

Verna knew all of her employees by their first names. Further, during the hiring process, she asked many questions concerning their personal lives. She felt that this was necessary if she was to provide them inspiration and, more importantly, guidance. Verna knew that most people have some kinds of personal problems. Since, other than high blood pressure and an occasional twinge of arthritis, she had none personally, she found great satisfaction in dealing with those of others. An enthusiastic reader of *Psychology Today*, she considered herself an excellent therapist.

Verna approached one of her stylists, Sylvia, who was busy with a customer. Verna casually inquired if Sylvia's husband's impotency was still a problem. This startled Sylvia somewhat since Verna's voice carried fairly well. While Sylvia cringed, customers listened as Verna discussed the interaction of personal hygiene, a high-fiber diet and sexual interest based on an article she had just read in *Psychology Today*. After a while, customers joined the conversation, offering their condolences and suggesting additional therapy varying from leather clothing to chicken soup.

Sylvia's problem "solved", Verna continued down the line of chairs to Monique who was administering a permanent wave. Verna noted, "Monique, you look tired today. Is there anything wrong?" Monique quickly responded that all was well. Verna insisted, "No, Monique, you need some rest. Take the rest of the day off; I'll get someone to finish up for you." Monique, who needed the income far more than rest, objected. Verna prevailed and led the resisting Monique out of the shop. "Don't go home by bus. Take a cab; be sure to take a cab. You shouldn't take a bus in your condition," Verna cautioned. Monique complied and took an available cab for a few blocks; then she caught a bus home. Once again, "Verna knew best".

Verna's office door was always open to employees. In fact, Verna encouraged members of "her family" to come to her with personal problems. Most long-term employees seemed reluctant to do this since they soon discovered that their personal problems became subjects of general discussion in the shop. However, the newer and younger employees did avail themselves of Verna's services. Their problems were often "whoppers"; these really stimluated Verna. Relying on her research in *Psychology Today* and occasionally the *National Inquirer*, Verna never failed to provide guidance regardless of the nature of the concern. Some of this advice resulted in disastrous consequences, but this did not deter Verna. After all, no doctor or psychiatrist had a perfect batting average, and Verna's services were free.

Verna's Beauty Emporium continued quite successfully until Verna's high blood pressure became a problem. She was required to spend less time at the shop. Her absence contributed to chaos since her employees were forced to operate without continuous supervision. Eventually, "Verna's family" began to dissipate. Verna's "children" were forced to face the cruel world without the inspiration and, more importantly, the guidance provided by their warm and caring "mother".

WHAT'S GOING ON HERE? WHY IS THIS HAPPENING?

Verna's style of leadership is called Benevolent Authoritative or Paternalistic (Chapter Two). Verna makes all of the decisions but treats subordinates in a kindly manner—somewhat like children. If subordinates are "childlike" in nature, this approach is likely to work. It certainly beats the Exploitative Authoritative style where the boss makes the decisions and treats subordinates badly. However, many adults resent being treated like children. If they are forced to, eventually they tend to act like children. In her efforts to "play mother", Verna is intruding into personal lives and probably exceeding her limits as a "therapist". Considering the nature and degree of some people's problems, this could be very dangerous.

COMMENT:

Some might challenge my criticism of Verna's style, noting, "Verna's a nice person who's trying to help her subordinates." They may have a point, but note that Verna's approach is used by totalitarian governments that tell their people what to do, what to think, whom to associate with, and whom, if anyone, to worship. Attempts to dominate people's <u>total</u> lives are, in my view, wrong.

WHAT SHOULD YOU DO IF YOU RECOGNIZE SOME OF THE CHARACTERISTICS OF VERNA MATERNA IN YOURSELF?

Give adults the respect they deserve; treat them like adults. Allow them to make decisions if they have the will and the skill. Be available to assist them on a confidential basis with personal problems or refer them to qualified specialists, but don't intrude into their personal lives unless invited. Avoid giving advice you're not qualified to give. If you're actually dealing with immature people, see if you can't help them "graduate" to greater maturity after a period of time.

WHAT SHOULD YOU DO IF YOU DISCOVER SOME OF THE CHARACTERISTICS OF VERNA MATERNA IN YOUR SUBORDINATES?

Explain that such behavior, while perhaps well-intentioned, doesn't normally help either the organization or its people. Encourage them to consider the points made in the previous paragraph.

WHAT SHOULD YOU DO IF YOU'RE WORKING FOR A BOSS WITH SOME OF THE CHARACTERISTICS OF VERNA MATERNA?

If you can live without making your own decisions and don't mind some interference in your personal life, working for a Verna might not be all that bad. However, prolonged exposure to a Verna-like boss is likely to make you a dependent person. Maybe you can convince Verna that you have no problems worth mentioning and that you can work on your own. If this isn't possible, I'd look for a job where you can use your mind and exercise the freedoms that should come with adulthood.

NOTES

[1]Michael Maccoby, *The Leader* (New York: Simon and Schuster, 1981), p. 23.

If you receive this through the mail, it is possible that someone is telling you something about your style of leadership as perceived by others. Perhaps you should read *Paul Malone's* first book on leadership, **Love 'Em and Lead 'Em** (Synergy Press, 3420 Holly Road, Annandale, VA 22003 — $10.95 plus $1.50 postage).

(FOLD HERE)

FROM: (Optional)

____

____

____

PLACE
STAMP
HERE

TO: ________________________________

____

____

____

(Staple Here)

CHAPTER NINETEEN

FUSS WITHOUT FOCUS

"Those who pole vault over mouse dropppings will inevitably hit their heads on something important." (BIG BOOK, Small Paul to the Nauseating Nitpickers, 73:99)

"The essence of a general's job is to assist in developing a clear sense of purpose . . . to keep the junk from getting in the way of important things."
General Walt Ulmer[1]

"But, nurse, Mr. Hoskins loves that dog very much; they've been together for years. Couldn't we bring him in for a few minutes? He's small. We could carry him in a dog carrier. My grandfather is very ill; it would do him a lot of good," pleaded the visitor at the BELCH-N-BELLO Nursing Home.

"Absolutely not!" firmly responded Mini Minutiae, shift nurse in the East Wing. "Dogs are noisy and dirty. Their nails scratch the wax on our linoleum. We'll show your grandfather a photograph of the dog."

Mini returned to her desk pleased that, once again, reason had triumphed over the foolishness that often creeps into life. She brushed a thread off her desk that, as usual, was completely bare—very tidy. Hers was a far cry from those of the other "disorganized" shift nurses that were piled with papers and files. Mini took pride in the comparison. It did not bother her that she

Abuse 'Em and Lose 'Em

was often unable to locate important records when she needed them.

Mini Minutiae liked order. According to Mini, "Life consists of many detailed activities. If you take care of the details, the big things will happen the right way." Mini's mind and eye constantly focused on the details. Often, the bigger things escaped her attention.

The mission of the BELCH-N-BELLO Nursing Home was to care in a professional, sympathetic and humane manner for elderly people unable to care for themselves. The nursing home management had become aware that the quality of this service declined in the East Wing when Mini was the shift nurse. But why? Mini was continually busy during her eight-hour tours. Further, the subordinates on her shift complained that she pushed them too hard. **The problem was not how hard people were working but what they were doing.**

"Hospital corners! Sheets folded precisely at 45-degree angles here and here," exclaimed Mini as she demonstrated making beds to two new employees. "These patients are careless; they let their beds get messed up during the day. It's up to you to maintain order." Mini then observed and corrected frequently as each new employee made a bed several times. This process took so much time that lunch was served late and cold in the East Wing that day.

Members of Mini's shift rushed to serve the cold lunch to the patients in the East Wing. Today was to be a busy one. A choral group of young people was scheduled to entertain the patients that afternoon. Patients had to be helped to the recreation room, a piano had to be moved, a public address system had to be set up.

Mini always seemed to get upset when she knew company was coming. In preparation, she inspected the rooms. To her dismay, many of the beds were rumpled. She rushed to one of the attendants who was helping a very feeble man eat his lunch and directed the attendant to straighten up all of the beds. "Hospital corners! I want hospital corners on every bed even if people are in them. Do it now; Mr. Dithers has had enough lunch anyway."

Actually, Mr. Dithers missed lunch that day.

The meal complete, the staff proceeded to set up the recreation room and prepare the patients for the entertainment UNTIL Mini detected a "major flaw" demanding immediate attention. It seemed that Mini had a particular preference regarding the storage of mops, brooms and pails in the utility areas of the East Wing. In fact, she had emphasized these procedures several times. To her dismay, she discovered that the mops, brooms and pails had been improperly stored in one of the utility rooms. Without hesitation, Mini gathered her entire staff and repeated her previous instructions regarding this "vital" matter. She then directed her staff to inspect all utility areas immediately and to rectify all discrepancies.

The "mop, broom and pail diversion" proved to be the undoing of plans to entertain the elderly people in the East Wing. When the choral group arrived, the piano hadn't been moved and the public address system hadn't been set up. Further, many of the patients were not ready to enter the recreation room. Mops, brooms and pails had taken priority over patients at a critical time. After waiting for 45 minutes and observing great confusion without resolution, the choral group departed resolving never again to volunteer to visit the BELCH-N-BELLO Nursing Home.

Somewhat shaken by the disorder, Mini returned to the tranquility of her immaculate desk and commented, "They don't make young people like they used to." She then rose and toured the utility rooms. To her immense satisfaction, the mops, brooms and pails were in order. As she walked past the door of a patient's room, she observed an elderly woman writhing in her bed apparently having a seizure. Alarmed, she rushed in and started rearranging the bed clothing, muttering, "Hospital corners!"

WHAT'S GOING ON HERE? WHY IS THIS HAPPENING?

Mini is a person who focuses on "activity traps", relatively inconsequential activities, at the expense of important mission-related objectives. Mini's priorities are screwed up. She inflicts these misdirected priorities on others; the organization and its customers suffer as a result. While details are important, some are far more important than others.

WHAT SHOULD YOU DO IF YOU RECOGNIZE SOME OF THE CHARACTERISTICS OF MINI MINUTIAE IN YOURSELF?

By all means, change your behavior. Find out WHY your organization exists, **your mission.** Determine the **objectives** that make mission accomplishment possible. Then decide **what must be done** to achieve those objectives. Finally, establish some **priorities**, giving the top priority to critical activities directly related to the mission. At all times, be alert to **eliminate senseless, unnecessary effort** (activity traps) so that your subordinates can focus on what's important.

WHAT SHOULD YOU DO IF YOU DISCOVER SOME OF THE CHARACTERISTICS OF MINI MINUTIAE IN YOUR SUBORDINATES?

If your subordinates are leaders, insist that they perform the steps listed in the previous paragraph. Make sure that **your** priorities are clearly stated; some of your subordinates may be doing stupid things because they think you want them done. Encourage your people to detect unnecessary activity, and reward those who do so.

WHAT SHOULD YOU DO IF YOU'RE WORKING FOR A BOSS WITH SOME OF THE CHARACTERISTICS OF MINI MINUTIAE?

Unfortunately, you must share your boss's priorities unless you can

GET THE "JUNK" OUT OF WORK

BE RUTHLESS!

convince him or her that he or she is wrong. Like it or not, one of your jobs is to please your boss. Everyone has a few biases and idiosyncrasies; that's tolerable. However, when these result in nonsense rather than sense, the organization and its people suffer, since mission accomplishment becomes secondary.

NOTES

[1] Tom Peters and Nancy Austin, *A Passion for Excellence* (New York: Random House, 1985), p. 285.

If you receive this through the mail, it is possible that someone is telling you something about your style of leadership as perceived by others. Perhaps you should read *Paul Malone's* first book on leadership, **Love 'Em and Lead 'Em** (Synergy Press, 3420 Holly Road, Annandale, VA 22003 — $10.95 plus $1.50 postage).

(FOLD HERE)

FROM: (Optional)

____

____

____

PLACE
STAMP
HERE

TO: ______________________________________

____

____

____

(Staple Here)

CHAPTER TWENTY

NUMERIZE 'EM AND DEHUMANIZE 'EM

"God didn't have a computer when he came up with this world. At least, it wasn't mentioned in the Bible." (BIG BOOK, Small Paul to the Systems Analysts, 18:38)

"America is suffering from an unhealthy emphasis on success as measured by The Numbers. The tendency to boil the world down into analytic abstractions distorts and oversimplifies the richness of life. It insists upon evaluating the world through ratings and lists, matrices and polls, the bottom line, winners and losers."
Norman Lear[1]

"Numbers, gentlemen, numbers! Everything in this world can be explained using numbers," philosophized Major General Seymour Digit as he looked up from a massive computer printout. General Digit was commanding a U.S. Army division during the Vietnam War. The scene was the weekly meeting of the commanders and staff officers of the division in the spacious underground division conference room. The front of the room was filled with many large charts, all containing quantitative data.

General Digit continued, "The numbers that count here are ENEMY KILLED; that's what we're paid to do. Let's take a look at the comparative data." The general turned to one of his brigade

US
US
ALL THE WORLD'S TRUTHS

commanders, "Colonel, your numbers are absolutely lousy! Your body count [number of enemy killed] is the lowest in the division. You're not doing your job!"

"But sir", responded the colonel defensively, "Intelligence reports indicate that the enemy has withdrawn from my brigade sector. There's just no one to shoot at other than friendly Vietnamese."

"I'm sick and tired of your excuses, Colonel", interrupted General Digit impatiently. "Just look at these other data. You aren't shooting your artillery ammunition, your venereal disease rate is up, your vehicular accident rate is high and your reenlistment rate is down. This constitutes irrefutable proof that your brigade is loving and carousing rather than fighting and, further, your morale stinks! I'm relieving you of your command!"

The colonel began to explain but decided against it. He was led out of the room in awkward silence. He was replaced by someone else to "play the numbers game".

Eventually, the war ended; everyone went home. Enemy body count had been high; many of the enemy had been killed. Some had been killed more than once so the numbers would look better. Despite this, the U.S. lost the war. It seemed that the factor that really counted–THE WILL TO FIGHT–hadn't been fully appreciated. Apparently, the enemy had it and we didn't. The problem was that it's tough to measure WILL by using numbers.

Naturally, the general was disappointed that the North Vietnamese won the war, but he reflected, "My body count was good–better than the others. I did my part." The two stars on each shoulder attested to his success as a military officer.

In college, Seymour Digit had been an outstanding student with particular talents in math, science and engineering. He had always been attracted to numbers. They seemed to bring precision to what otherwise appeared to be an uncertain, complex and chaotic world. As a junior officer, he put his skills to productive use. He determined what numbers were important to his bosses and then focused all of his energies toward achieving those numerical targets to the exclusion of all other considerations. He discovered ways to manipulate numbers to his own advantage. When venereal disease was the thing to avoid, his troops developed "urinary tract irritations of unknown origin". Whereas he wasn't particularly popular with his troops, his units were always tops regarding the numbers that really counted. Even in his personal life Seymour was very competitive. When he married the first time, he determined that evidence of marital success was a function of the number of children conceived. However, his wife failed to appreciate his imposition of quotas and told him to go play with his calculator while she took off with a long-haired pacifist hippie.

Seymour Digit was considered an extraordinary staff officer. His studies and reports, replete with reams of quantitative data, were the pride of the Pentagon. When some questioned his use of numbers, he turned to ratios–numbers divided by other numbers. When ratios also seemed too simplistic, he developed ratios of ratios and then complex mathematical models–all devised to reduce the ambiguities of life to logical, rational precision. Sometimes, he "cheated" a bit and inserted his own subjective views into these models. However, since they were very complicated, no one seemed to know this or really care. Naturally, Seymour applauded the arrival of calculators and later computers. His few close personal friends were the "computer weenies"–those who tended the computers. When he finally got his opportunity to command in Vietnam, he discovered an extraordinary opportunity to reduce the complexities of war to an elaborate and super-sophisticated "numbers game". It worked for him.

When the war ended, General Digit engaged in an intricate quantitative analysis of his future opportunities in the Army. Concluding that his skills would be appreciated more on the outside, he retired and established a management consulting firm. His specialty was helping "sick" organizations get well. Naturally, his focus was on the numbers. In fact, he claimed that all that was necessary for the analysis of a firm was a review of its numbers—visits with the firm and discussions with its people were time-consuming and unnecessary. Some of his "patients" got better—but only for a while. His "therapy" proved to be a "band-aid approach" rather than long-lasting in nature. Eventually, the consulting business began to die off; it seemed that there's more to life than numbers. Meanwhile, Seymour Digit took up golf, AND FOCUSED ON THE NUMBERS.

WHAT'S GOING ON HERE? WHY IS THIS HAPPENING?

Seymour is suffering from a severe case of "numberungus"—a blind reverence for numbers (don't look for this word in the dictionary—I made it up).[2] Many people seek to understand the bewildering complexities of life. Some turn to religion, others to science. Apparently, Seymour has concluded that quantitative analysis holds the key to interpreting events and predicting the future—including human behavior. Considering the explosion of knowledge and the enhanced capabilities of computers to help digest that knowledge, Seymour has a point—but he goes too far. He assumes that everything has a scientific explanation amenable to rational, scientific analysis. In Seymour's world, the "arts" or the "fine arts" don't really matter much; things that can't be counted or analyzed scientifically are relatively inconsequential. In his book, *The Leader*, Michael Maccoby notes that "What is lacking for the education of leaders in our culture is education in the humanities, first of all in clear writing and speaking, but also in religion, ethical philosophy, in-depth psychology and history."[3]

WHAT SHOULD YOU DO IF YOU RECOGNIZE SOME OF THE CHARACTERISTICS OF SEYMOUR DIGIT IN YOURSELF?

First off, let me say that you have lots of company; there are plenty of Seymour Digits around. Many of them are products of highly specialized technical educations and professions where their analytical abilities and unique skills are needed desperately. Because they do well in their specialties they are often rewarded. Frequently, their rewards involve promotions to supervisory positions. Many are not well-prepared to deal with the "fine art" of leadership.

My advice is to recognize that people have both **rational** and **emotional** dimensions. Rational processes are predictable; emotional responses often are not. **Have you ever been in LOVE? Do you remember the silly things you did because you LOVED another human being?** Conversely, HATE, another emotional response, can be a powerful motivator; witness the Holocaust. Remember that each person is behaving "rationally" according to his or her unique value system (which may be very different from yours). If you have real problems dealing with this, either (1) get some help from an experienced leader, (2) take some courses on leadership and human behavior or (3) find a deputy who is adept at dealing with the human dimension.

WHAT SHOULD YOU DO IF YOU DISCOVER SOME OF THE CHARACTERISTICS OF SEYMOUR DIGIT IN YOUR SUBORDINATES?

These people often are excellent STAFF workers. STAFF people provide advice, services and support to the LINE workers **who make most of the decisions and are responsible for the performance of subordinates.** However, if you have LINE subordinates whose orientations are exclusively analytical, you're likely to have problems. In such cases, my advice is similar to that in the preceding paragraph. Convince them that there is no mathematical model that can analyze the needs and predict the behavior of each and every human being.

WHAT SHOULD YOU DO IF YOU'RE WORKING FOR A BOSS WITH SOME OF THE CHARACTERISTICS OF SEYMOUR DIGIT?

By all means give your boss what he wants, the proper numbers. At the same time, if you have subordinates, recognize both their rational and emotional aspects. If you win the confidence of your boss, it is possible that you can convince him or her that some important things in life are unquantifiable. However, since most people make up their minds about life in general before they're middle aged, this is probably a "long shot".

NOTES

[1]Tom Peters and Nancy Austin, *A Passion for Excellence* (New York: Random House, 1985), p. 415.

[2]Paul B. Malone III, *Love 'Em and Lead 'Em* (Annandale, VA: Synergy Press, 1986), p. 126.

[3]Michael Maccoby, *The Leader* (New York: Simon and Schuster, 1981), p. 231.

If you receive this through the mail, it is possible that someone is telling you something about your style of leadership as perceived by others. Perhaps you should read *Paul Malone's* first book on leadership, **Love 'Em and Lead 'Em** (Synergy Press, 3420 Holly Road, Annandale, VA 22003 — $10.95 plus $1.50 postage).

(FOLD HERE)

FROM: (Optional)

____

____

____

PLACE
STAMP
HERE

TO: ____________________________________

____

____

____

(Staple Here)

PART C

CONCLUSIONS

CHAPTER TWENTY-ONE

SO WHAT?

"True leadership exists when one imperfect human being (complete with his or her share of 'warts') creates a situation wherein other human beings, also imperfect, want to stretch and grow in a common cause that benefits all while each person senses a warm glow of satisfaction." (BIG BOOK: Small Paul to the People Movers and Shakers, 21:15)

"With champions, success lies in the journey, not the destination."
Harvey Mackay[1]

"Leadership is the privilege to have the responsibility to direct the actions of others in carrying out the purposes of the organization, at varying levels of authority and with accountability for both successful and failed endeavors."
Wess Roberts[2]

Part C, the final part of this book, consists of this one chapter. It is an attempt to bring a message together and make reading this book a cost-effective investment for you. If you've stuck with this book so far, you've waded through eighteen brief "horror stories"—perhaps exaggerated and a bit unrealistic, but all with real messages. The question is, how can this experience be put to productive use?

Mistakes are great ways to learn. However, mistakes can be costly. If you can learn from the mistakes of others, you're likely to be way ahead. No person is "perfect". However, those who are aware of their imperfections and attempt to reduce their effects have a good chance to succeed.

HAVE ALL OF THE INEPT STYLES OF LEADERSHIP BEEN COVERED?

Absolutely not! Full coverage would result in a much thicker book and an expired author. Some additional "corrupt" styles that exist and persist that were considered but not included in detail are listed below:

- "THE SILENT ONE"--The leader who keeps his subordinates totally uninformed and tells them nothing about the organizational mission, goals and objectives. This is referred to by some as the "Mushroom Treatment"--feed 'em horse manure and keep 'em in the dark.
- "THE DO IT MY WAY LEADER"--The leader who is a workaholic and who insists on doing all of the creative work himself while his subordinates watch.
- "THE IDEA THIEF"--The leader who "picks the brains" of his subordinates and then takes full credit for their creative ideas.
- "THE PERFECTIONIST"--The leader who is totally intolerant of mistakes and allows none in the organization.
- "THE CHAMELEON"--The leader who changes his style frequently, all the way from authoritative to participative, and totally confuses subordinates.
- "THE PHONY"--The leader who professes one style of leadership but practices something different.

CAN WE GIVE THIS EXAMINATION SOME STRUCTURE?

If you're interested, turn to the worksheets on the following pages and rate yourself with regard to the styles described in Part B plus those mentioned above. Be as candid as you can, recognizing that you probably like yourself and can be "blind" to your imperfections. Recognize that leading people is something like hanging wallpaper. **You can never achieve absolute perfection, but you can work on reducing or perhaps concealing your imperfections.** The fact that you are concerned and are working on it is very important. If you want to "get tough", you might ask one of your subordinates who has observed you for some time to rate you using the same format.

SUGGESTION: COMPARE YOUR OWN STYLE OF LEADERSHIP TO THOSE LISTED ON THE NEXT FOUR PAGES, USING ONE OF THE FOLLOWING TERMS–NEVER, SELDOM, OCCASIONALLY, FREQUENTLY, ALWAYS.

CHECK OUT YOUR LEADERSHIP "ZITS"

EVERYONE'S GOT THEM

CHAPTER	"VILLAIN"	STYLE	RESPONSE
Three	Richard Devius	Leader mainpulates people and leads using lies, deceit, and treachery.	
Four	Norma Proforma	Leader creates an environment of impersonality and manages "by the book".	
Five	Aaron Arshoal	Leader makes all of the decisions and treats subordinates like dirt.	
Six	Philo Philander	Leader engages in sexual harassment of subordinates.	
Seven	Ignacio Incompetenti	Leader is basically incompetent–doesn't know his or her job.	
Eight	Nardo Narcissy	Leader uses status in the organization to feed his or her ego.	

CHAPTER	"VILLAIN"	STYLE	RESPONSE
Nine	Phoebus Laissezfaire	Leader refuses to exercise his or her authority; lets subordinates "do their thing".	
Ten	Abner Slack	Leader is totally unconcerned for either the mission of the organization or the welfare of its members.	
Eleven	Bella Cose	Leader relies on emotional outbursts to influence subordinate behavior and rules through tantrums.	
Twelve	E. Studley Strump	Leader establishes an organizational "class system" and expects total conformity.	
Thirteen	Burton Buffoon	Leader engages in foolish behavior and humiliates subordinates.	
Fourteen	Tess Terone	Female leader adopts the behavior of a coarse man when exercising authority.	

CHAPTER	"VILLAIN"	STYLE	RESPONSE
Fifteen	Kassandra Kaos	Leader considers every event a crisis and overreacts while creating chaos in the organization.	
Sixteen	Blair Despair	Pessimistic leader contributes to gloom in the organization.	
Seventeen	Pam Demonium	Leader encourages communication within the organization but is unable or unwilling to make decisions.	
Eighteen	Verna Materna	Leader makes all of the decisions but treats subordinates in a kindly manner–much like children.	
Nineteen	Mini Minutiae	Leader focuses on "activity traps", relatively unimportant activities, while critical, mission-related concerns are ignored.	
Twenty	Seymour Digit	Leader is "mesmerized" by the scientific method and quantitative analysis to the degree that considerations that are unquantifiable are disregarded.	

CHAPTER	"VILLAIN"	STYLE	RESPONSE
Twenty-One	"The Silent One"	Leader keeps subordinates totally "in the dark" regarding the organizational mission, goals and objectives.	
Twenty-One	"The Do-It-My-Way Leader"	Leader is a workaholic who insists on doing all of the creative work while others watch.	
Twenty-One	"The Idea Thief"	Leader "picks the brains" of subordinates and then introduces their creative ideas as his or her own.	
Twenty-One	"The Perfection-ist"	Leader insists on perfection in all things and tolerates no mistakes.	
Twenty-One	"The Chameleon"	Leader continually changes his or her style of leadership, all the way from authoritative to participative, and confuses subordinates.	
Twenty-One	"The Phony"	Leader professes a participative style of leadership while behaving in an authoritative manner.	

If you consider the "drill" on the previous pages somewhat superficial, you might consider an alternative approach that requires a little more thought. Select one or two of the leadership styles identified in the book that, to a degree, reflect your behavior. Then, respond to the following questions in some depth:

- Why am I behaving this way?
- What effect, if any, does my style have on my subordinates?
- What, if anything, do I plan to do about it?

IS THERE ANOTHER WAY TO LOOK AT LEADERSHIP?

By all means. Remember that there are two perspectives of the leader: (1) what the leader thinks he or she is and (2) what the subordinates see. Since most leaders are also followers of someone else, they might benefit from (1) evaluating their bosses and then (2) thinking about the same evaluations from the perspectives of their own subordinates. I've listed below some statements regarding the environment of leadership that I consider appropriate. Coincidentally, there are nine, the same as the number of **Malone's Commandments of Leadership** mentioned in Chapter Two. There are many such lists prepared by others designed to accomplish the same purpose. I suggest that you respond to the statements below using the following entries–**AGREE, SOMEWHAT AGREE, UNDECIDED, SOMEWHAT DISAGREE and DISAGREE.** Then, think about how **your** subordinates would respond to the same statements.

HOW DO YOU VIEW YOUR BOSS?

1. My boss "stands for" values, to include ethical standards, that subordinates understand, accept and respect, lives by them, and transmits them into the "culture" of the organization.

2. My boss demonstrates loyalty to subordinates and a willingness to "go to bat" for them when they're in the right, regardless of the consequences.

3. My boss treats subordinates with the dignity and respect that mature adults deserve and designs meaningful work with this in mind.

4. My boss allows subordinates to work to the limit of their individual capacities and encourages and supports their growth and development.

5. My boss encourages communication and creative thought and recognizes and rewards subordinates equitably according to their individual contributions to the organization.

6. My boss lets subordinates know what's going on in the organization, including how they're expected to contribute, and WHY.

7. My boss creates an organizational environment that is optimistic, stimulating, rewarding and, whenever possible, FUN.

8. My boss demonstrates a genuine concern for the welfare of subordinates and a willingness to assist those with problems.

9. My boss generates confidence among subordinates through an ability to interpret events and trends and to guide the organization into the uncertainty of a changing world.

IS LEADING ANY FUN?

I think leading can be extraordinarily satisfying, but I'm biased. Rather than discussing this further, let me refer you to the photograph on the next page. Forgive me for waving my family at you, but I feel that the picture has a message. It shows our older son, Paul B. Malone IV, then a captain in the U. S. Army, commanding his company of 160 rompin'-stompin' paratroopers in the field.[3] He's the little guy in the left center. If you'll study his face closely, you'll note a smile. This is the smile of satisfaction that goes with leading well. Whereas it's very unlikely that Paul will ever be a rich man (unless this book sells well and he inherits a "gold mine"), he will experience the intense personal satisfactions (intrinsic rewards) that go with getting a job done well and, at the same time, helping his people to become **more and better.** According to my value system, this beats a huge bankroll all to pieces. If your value system differs from mine substantially, maybe that's a signal you should consider.

IS LEADING FOR EVERYBODY?

Since nothing is for everybody, the obvious answer is "No". Some claim that leadership ability is a "natural" talent—either you have it or you don't. I disagree. Leadership ability can be compared to athletic ability. Some people are "natural" athletes; others are less gifted. However, with training, practice and determination, almost all can improve their abilities to some degree. Harvey Mackay, the author of *Beware the Naked Man Who Offers You His Shirt*, agrees, ". . . Human-relations skills can be learned. . . . There isn't a manager from the top on down who couldn't improve in this area. Caring is contagious. Help spread it around."[4]

On the other hand, I think some people should avoid accepting the responsibilities of leadership.

- If you're uncomfortable using **power** (the ability to attain dominance over others) and being **responsible** for the behavior of others, perhaps you should follow. Often, practice following can give you the confidence you need to lead later on.
- If you really don't like most people, I suggest that you work alone. There are many very satisfying jobs where this is possible.
- If you're a totally selfish person, that selfishness will show. I don't think that such a person will stimulate loyalty among subordinates. Of course, some such people **manage** and become rich and famous.
- If you have neither the time nor the energy to commit yourself to the organization and its people, don't become its leader. Leading can be extraordinarily challenging, demanding and time-consuming. Even excellent "natural leaders" can perform poorly if they're working only part-time or at low energy levels.
- Finally, if you have a totally corrupt value system, you're a potential hazard. Effective leaders with such "qualities" have made the world and its people **less**. Please don't lead; go to a monastery and get better before you meet the Lord.

WHO CARES? DOES LEADERSHIP REALLY MAKE A DIFFERENCE?

It should be obvious that I think it does. Perhaps a few truly dedicated professionals can operate at maximum efficiency regardless of the supervisory environment. However, most people are influenced by their perceptions of how and why the boss operates as he or she does. Most people must join organizations–**artificial structures designed by other people**–in order to earn their daily bread. In the process, they willingly give up some freedom–freedom they value highly. While a limitless variety of things can happen, the cartoons on the next page illustrate two extremes.

In the case of **ineffective leadership**, their enthusiasm, energies and creative instincts are sapped by the insensitive and often inhuman characteristics of the leadership style–a tragic process for both the organization and its people. The result is often associated with **ENTROPY**–the tendency to decay and die.

A very different result can be achieved with **effective leadership.** Again, people give up some freedom in order to earn a living. However, with **effective leadership**, there can be something akin to an "implosion" of energy–the "synergistic" or "two plus two equals five" effect. With **effective leadership**, there can be commitment, common purpose, organizational enthusiasm and extraordinary creativity throughout the entire workforce. Very often the result is the success of the organization and, equally important, the satisfaction of its members.

CONCLUDING COMMENTS

Some will observe that the author of this book is **optimistic** regarding people. **I hope it shows.** Others will conclude that he is **unrealistic** regarding people. **I hope they're wrong.** I recognize that much of what I have written doesn't apply well to the "casualties" of an affluent Post-Industrial Society–those unfortunates who are committed to hate, drugs, crime and the like. On the other end of the scale, my message won't make much sense to those totally committed to personal greed regardless of cost to others. However, I am convinced that there is a huge "middle mass" of good people who have a tremendous **need to be excellent** and who are willing to work within the established system. A few with talent and lots of luck can make it on their own. However, since very few things nowadays can be accomplished by people working alone, most must work in organizations. In the process,

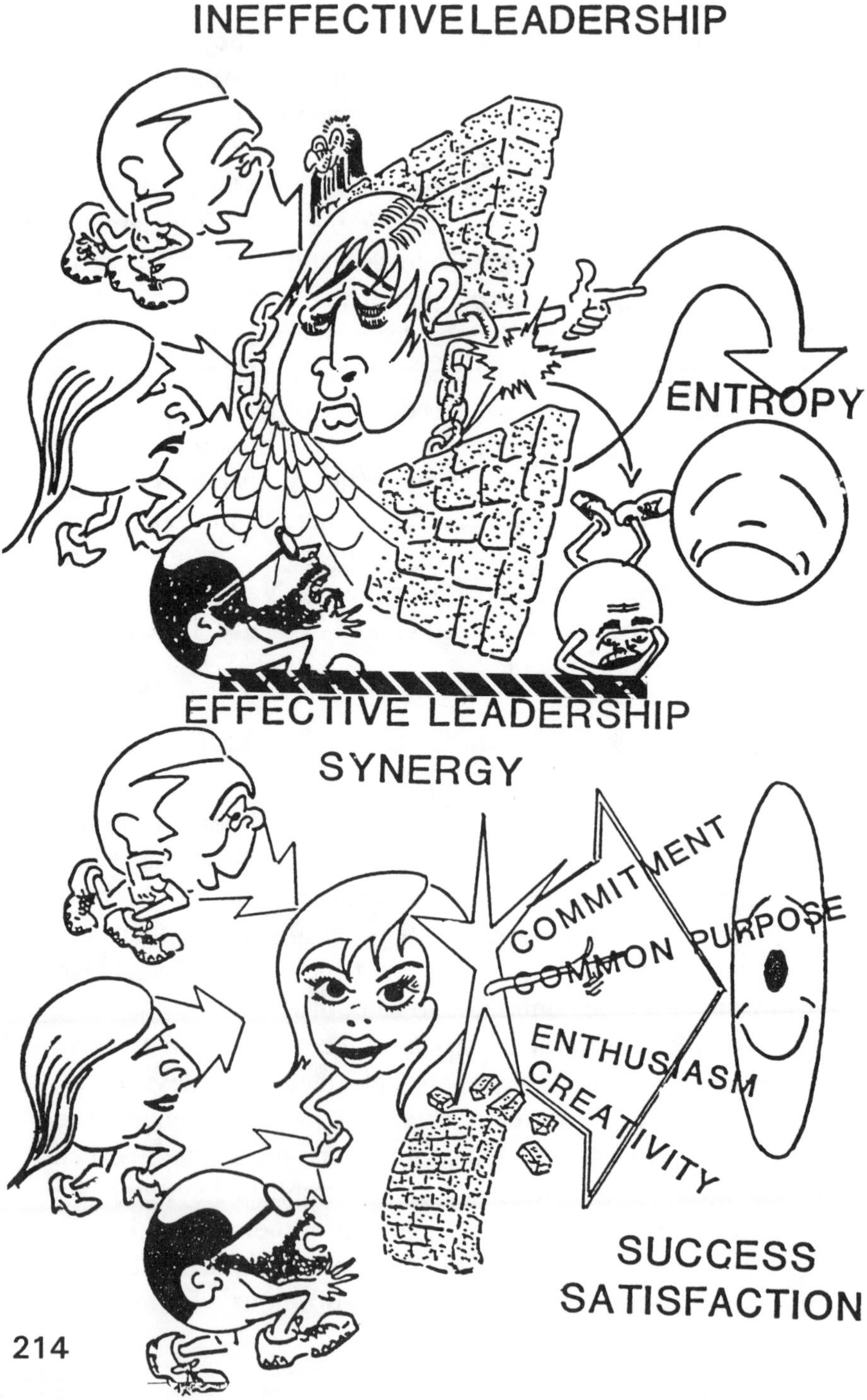
INEFFECTIVE LEADERSHIP
ENTROPY
EFFECTIVE LEADERSHIP
SYNERGY
COMMITMENT
COMMON PURPOSE
ENTHUSIASM
CREATIVITY
SUCCESS
SATISFACTION

they must make some sacrifices. The question now is, **what is the price and what are the rewards?** Those who are **managed or led poorly**, treated as inanimate cogs in some sort of organizational machine, are usually only **physically involved in their work** and doing just enough to get by. In the process, their **need to be excellent** is ignored. For those who are **led effectively**, another scenario is possible. They can become "motivated". My definition of "motivated" is being **physically, mentally and emotionally involved in their work; committed to improving performance.** In the process, their **need to be excellent** can be satisfied. To me, that's the "spice" of life. Do I sound like a dreamer? Walt Disney noted that "if you can dream it, you can do it".[5] Effective leaders can serve as the world's "dream actuators". At this point, I just can't resist closing with these often-quoted lines from George Bernard Shaw's *Man and Superman* that seem so appropriate for practicing and aspiring leaders:

> This is the true joy of life, the being used for a purpose recognized by yourself as a mighty one; the being a force of nature instead of a feverish selfish little clod of ailments and grievances complaining that the world will not devote itself to making you happy.[6]

NOTES

[1]Harvey Mackay, *Beware the Naked Man Who Offers You His Shirt* (New York: William Morrow and Company, Inc., 1990), p. 366.

[2]Wess Roberts, *Leadership Secrets of Attila the Hun* (New York: Warner Books, 1985), p. xiv.

[3]Soldiers of Company C, 1st Battalion, 325th Airborne Infantry, 82nd Airborne Division, engaged in field training in Mississippi.

[4]Mackay, *Naked Man*, p. 149.

[5]Warren Bennis and Burt Nanus, *Leaders* (New York: Harper & Row, 1985), p. 33.

[6]George Bernard Shaw, *Man and Superman* (Baltimore: Penguin, 1973), p. 84.

ABOUT THE AUTHOR

Paul Malone (the one without facial hair) integrates a 30-year military career and twelve years in academia into a book on a vital subject that is contemporary, practical and entertaining. This book is a sequel to his first book on leadership, *Love 'Em and Lead 'Em*, which he published himself (Synergy Press is his home). That book has been reprinted four times and has been adopted for many education and training programs. It is currently being published in Chinese and Czechoslovak versions.

Paul's interest in leadership began when he was a cadet at West Point and continued throughout his military career as a paratrooper, Ranger and Army Aviator. He had many opportunities to lead and has made his share of mistakes. During his first tour in the Vietnam War, he received a severe gunshot wound while flying his helicopter and directing the extraction from the jungle of an ambushed infantry battalion. This wound led to a reorientation of his military career from combat unit assignments to executive-level education and development. He retired from the Army in the grade of colonel. His military service was recognized by three awards of the Legion of Merit, the Distinguished Flying Cross, and numerous other decorations including the Purple Heart.

Paul's interest in writing on the subject of leadership was stimulated when he earned a Doctor of Business Administration degree and taught at the National Defense University in Washington, D.C. He has taught leadership- and management-related subjects at the undergraduate, graduate and executive levels both at the National Defense University and, later after retirement from the Army, at George Washington University where he is now a member of the faculty of the School of Business and Public Management. While at George Washington University, he has served twice in the capacity of Assistant Dean.

Paul's fondness for innovation, fun and humor first became apparent at West Point where his cartooning poked gentle fun at "the system". He has attempted to integrate this philosophy into his teaching. His efforts in this area, not without mishap, have resulted in a speaking style characterized by unlimited enthusiasm, occasional irreverence, and, in general, highly satisfied customers. Listed in *Who's Who in Professional Speaking*, Paul has addressed a wide variety of audiences in the United States and in other countries. Whether writing or speaking, Paul seeks to transmit a vital message in an inspirational and stimulating manner.

The dogs with Paul are family Lhasa Apsos. The white dog, King Tut, is dyed green each March in honor of Saint Patrick's Day.

ORDER FORM

TO: SYNERGY PRESS
3420 HOLLY ROAD
ANNANDALE, VA 22003

TELEPHONE: (703) 573 0909

Enclosed is a check for ________ . Please send me the following by Paul Malone:

(___) copy(ies) of *Abuse 'Em and Lose 'Em* (paperback only). Price: $14.95 for book plus $1.60 for shipping of one book and $.40 for each additional book.

(___) copy(ies) of *Love 'Em and Lead 'Em*. Price: $10.95 for book plus $1.50 for shipping of one book and $.30 for each additional book.

....

____ I'd like my book(s) signed by the author.

____ Please send me information concerning quantity order discounts and hard cover rates (*Love 'Em and Lead 'Em* only hard cover).

____ I can't wait 2-3 weeks for book rate. Enclosed is $3.00 per book for First Class Mail.

....

I understand that I may return the book(s) undamaged for a full refund if not satisfied.

NAME:____

ADDRESS:____

____**ZIP**____________